ALIMENTARI

LINDA + PAUL JONES

ALIMENTARI

*Salads + other classics from
a little deli that grew*

hardie grant books

CONTENTS

FOREWORD

Some places transcend function. They are more than the sum of their parts. While it might appear that the Brunswick Street Alimentari is nothing out of the ordinary – just another café serving food and coffee on a street full of cafés serving food and coffee – it's actually quite extraordinary.

Alimentari is one of those rare places that inspires fierce loyalty and a sense of ownership in its clientele. It's a landmark that maintains a steadfastly no-bullshit attitude on a street that has always liked to prostrate itself at the feet of fads. It's solidly rooted in the old-school multicultural, bohemian Fitzroy landscape, a meeting place for locals and ex-locals where heartache and triumph, happiness and failure, beginnings, endings and the grind of the middle are picked apart, laughed about, cried over, solved, forgotten and remembered over meatball wraps, piadina and haloumi pies.

I know all this because Alimentari has been a part of my life for years, mostly due to friendship but also because of a chronic addiction to sambusic.

I first heard about it one night when Dolores and Linda came into Marios, where I was working at the time, to celebrate signing the lease for their new business. They showed me a picture of an old-school Italian alimentari, all well-worn wooden shelves stuffed with cheese and bread and salami, the café equivalent of a spirit animal that would accommodate their Italian and Lebanese heritages. And while the Brunswick Street Alimentari and its larger bustling Smith Street sibling have grown and morphed into something quite different to that small rustic ideal, at its core the business has stayed true to that original vision. It's kept its heart. And its cred.

Alimentari was born the same year as my daughter and as a baby she spent time behind the counter, swept up by Dolores who would continue making coffee with my kid resting on one hip, usually chewing on something Dolores had handed her that if I'd tried to make her eat would have led to a nuclear scale meltdown. When a place reminds you of your now-grown kid as a happy baby, it's kind of like family.

I also nursed a severely broken heart there and if I ever write that self-help book about getting through the seemingly endless damp moping stage, I'll have to include several chapters on the unbeatable combination of chicken schnitzel wraps and kind, blunt, hilarious commentary from Linda and Dolores.

When Dolores died she left a huge, unfillable Dolores-shaped hole in the lives of many people. It's still there, years later. But Alimentari was undiminished. It didn't continue as a shrine to Dolores, more a repository of her particular energy and attitude that always kept things moving, kept things interesting. That didn't just happen though. It was nurtured, obviously by Linda but also by her husband Paul.

Paul's cheffing background had been in restaurants not cafés, but he instinctively understood the essence of Alimentari. And while instrumental in expanding the repertoire and the acreage of the business, he's also been mindful of the essential calibration – the one that harks back to that old photo – that always put heart and flavour and integrity before the essential but more prosaic business of making money.

I'm glad Linda and Paul have decided to share the place in print. It's bittersweet to be reminded of Dolores but we'd all rather remember. It's also slightly unsettling to see the recipes for some of my favourite things released for general consumption. But more good food in the world is never a bad thing. And that makes Alimentari a very good thing indeed.

Michael Harden

INTRODUCTION

Dolores and I were high school friends. We lost touch after school but rekindled our relationship years later through our mutual friend Theresa. Fitzroy was our neighbourhood. We lived there together in the late nineties, frequenting Brunswick Street hangouts such as The Night Cat and Gypsy Bar.

Dolores (or Dee, as she was known by many) and I believed the street lacked a good continental deli. There had been a small mum-and-dad shop that served huge slabs of cheese and charcuterie on thick slices of bread. It was a local favourite but had sadly closed down, leaving a pretty big hole.

The idea for an 'alimentari' (which is essentially an Italian grocery store) came about after I'd travelled through Italy and pretty much eaten my way from alimentari to alimentari. The concept of being able to pick out a bread roll and choose from the magnificent ingredients to build my own panini was amazing. Certainly a far cry from the cucumber, shredded carrot and sliced cheese available back home at the time. Dolores had extensive experience working at a deli in Port Melbourne and our mutual love of food inspired us to take our vision to the next level.

So in 1998, we planned to open a small delicatessen on Brunswick Street. It would be rustic and cosy with shelves full of Italian and Middle Eastern groceries. It was important our backgrounds – mine Lebanese and Dee's Italian – be well represented.

Needless to say, our dream preceded our finances. We pretty much did everything back to front. We trawled Brunswick Street looking for the perfect venue and we eventually found it: Clones Menswear at number 251.

Those around at the time may recall the heads mounted onto the outside wall. The building had the exact vintage feel that we wanted (our vision at the time was a 1950s Italian deli – as it still is). We hunted down the agent who informed us that the tenants' lease was coming up. So we jumped at the opportunity and figured we'd get the money after we'd taken over the lease. Except no bank would give us a loan: two women in their early 30s with no man involved? No way.

We began renovating and trying to find capital at the same time. We smashed down walls, painted 18-foot-high ceilings while standing on rickety ladders, searched for stock, negotiated a free coffee machine and found a beautiful 1960s deli cabinet (which is still going strong) from a second-hand store in Richmond. Gingham curtains, dark wooden shelving and lino flooring – we thought it looked amazing. Lavazza gave us two collapsible outdoor tables and chairs, which we used as our indoor furniture.

Still no money. Dee's brother Joe came to the rescue and our silent partner at the time came up with the rest. But it still wasn't enough. So, there was a lot of of stalling and negotiating to get around tradies and suppliers. And our friends helped us along the way, cleaning and stocking shelves.

The night before we opened, Dee and I sat on the floor and admired our business. We were so proud, tired, nervous and excited. We began to jokingly role-play our first customer interaction.

"Good morning, can I help you?"

"Yes, I would like a focaccia."

"Certainly, have here or take away?"

It was at that point, at 11 o'clock on the night before our big opening, that we realised we had no plates! So off to the supermarket we went, armed with a cheque book, not knowing if it was ready to use or not. Needless to say, we were pretty shattered the next morning. But we did it, with plates.

After a while the two tables turned into a couple more. The deli was slowly becoming known as the place to come for a quick, fresh, delicious meal. It was, and still is, a place you could come to by yourself and feel comfortable, and know that you would most likely end up bumping into a friend. Our end of Brunswick Street was where locals would shop and hang out. We were fortunate to become part of the local fabric and we loved it. We were a part of a friendly and supportive network of traders such as Black Cat, Vasette, Thomas Gannan, Guernica and Jasper Coffee.

Dee and I worked seven days a week. The strain of working 12 hours a day began to take its toll. We could barely look at each other without fighting. So, in our infinite wisdom, we decided that if this was to be our life for the foreseeable future, then we still needed to live it. Our favourite club, Honky Tonks, became our regular haunt. I know a few locals who would be able to recall many a morning seeing Dolores driving the coffee machine looking magnificent with her shades on and me dying in the corner.

At this point we were offering five different panini, and every morning my mother Manera would deliver hot Lebanese pies, kibbeh and felafel. We were slowly becoming busier and we knew we had to offer more. However the thought of letting someone else in and paying wages was pretty scary. We decided to employ a friend of ours, Marina, who is an amazing cook. We were able to offer a soup and a pasta, as well as a few extras such as our tomato bruschetta and our BEST, which are still on the menu today.

We were a family, and we began to recruit like-minded people who loved hospitality and food. We soon employed a wonderful local guy called Drew, and Dee's family members Sassie and Josh. They all embodied what we stood for – they loved food, people and having a good time. We knew every person who walked through that door. To this day, I feel that is still what makes Alimentari so special.

In early 2005 I met and fell madly in love with my now husband and business partner Paul Jones. Unfortunately, at the same time, our lives were changed forever when Dee was diagnosed with cancer.

Dolores decided cancer wasn't going to slow her down and that she still wanted to be a part of the business. While I stayed at home with my first child, Dolores ran the place. She would have her chemo, come in with the chemo pack strapped to her waist and rock that coffee machine.

I OFTEN GET ASKED ABOUT OUR INITIAL BUSINESS PLAN. WE NEVER HAD ONE. FOR THE PAST 18 YEARS THE BUSINESS HAS TOLD US WHAT TO DO. THEY KEY WAS, AND STILL IS, TO LISTEN TO IT.

Dolores *was* Alimentari and for five years, she fought a brave battle. Dee began to pull back around 2008 and Paul stepped in.

Throughout all the bickering, hard work and constant demands of running a business, Dee and I had become sisters. She was at my side on my wedding day, and she is godmother to my daughter Aziza. She was with me through the difficult birth of my son Axel and through every other major moment in my life. Unfortunately, Dee passed away on June 19, 2010. To this day, her presence is felt and I can still hear her voice in every decision being made (I won't repeat what she's saying though!).

Paul is an amazing chef. I credit him for helping make Alimentari into what it is today, and this book is full of recipes that have been developed and executed by him. Over time we expanded our menu to take-home meals, knocked down walls, got rid of our back room and took full advantage of the beautiful space we inhabit.

By updating the kitchen, extending the seating area and taking the menu to new heights, Paul helped Alimentari grow up and be taken a little more seriously. Through his vision, Alimentari pioneered the extensive sale of the quality salads which we are known for today. At this point, Amit and Kaji began working with us and Paul trained the boys from humble beginnings as kitchen hands, to eventually become the backbone of our Brunswick Street kitchen.

As a married couple with young children, working together every day has its challenges, and it can literally make or break your relationship. But Paul is a wonderful man who is the most amazing father and partner – both in life and in business.

Keeping up with the demand for our range of take-home meals was behind the expansion to Smith Street. At the time, we were in partnership with my close friend Meaghan running Gorski & Jones. The business next door closed down and Paul thought it would be a great space for our food store. The wall came down and Smith Street Alimentari was born.

In 2004 we employed a sweet 17-year-old girl from Kerang by the name of Ashlee. Ash grew to love Alimentari as much as I did. She got it. So, when I was home with my young children, it gave me peace of mind knowing Ash was there. I'm thrilled that Ash is now our partner at Brunswick Street Alimentari, and if it wasn't for her, Smith Street would not have been possible.

Alimentari has almost become its own entity. I often get asked about our initial business plan. We never had one. For the past 18 years the business has told us what to do. The key was, and still is, to listen to it. We never had a publicity machine, we never really had that many reviews or write-ups. We've had the support of our community. It's been a slow growth, which is maybe the reason for our success.

This book is not about reinventing the wheel. It's a collection of simple recipes, some of which have been on our menu since we first opened. It's been a wonderful and emotional journey for me to write it.

I hope you enjoy my story.

Linda Jones

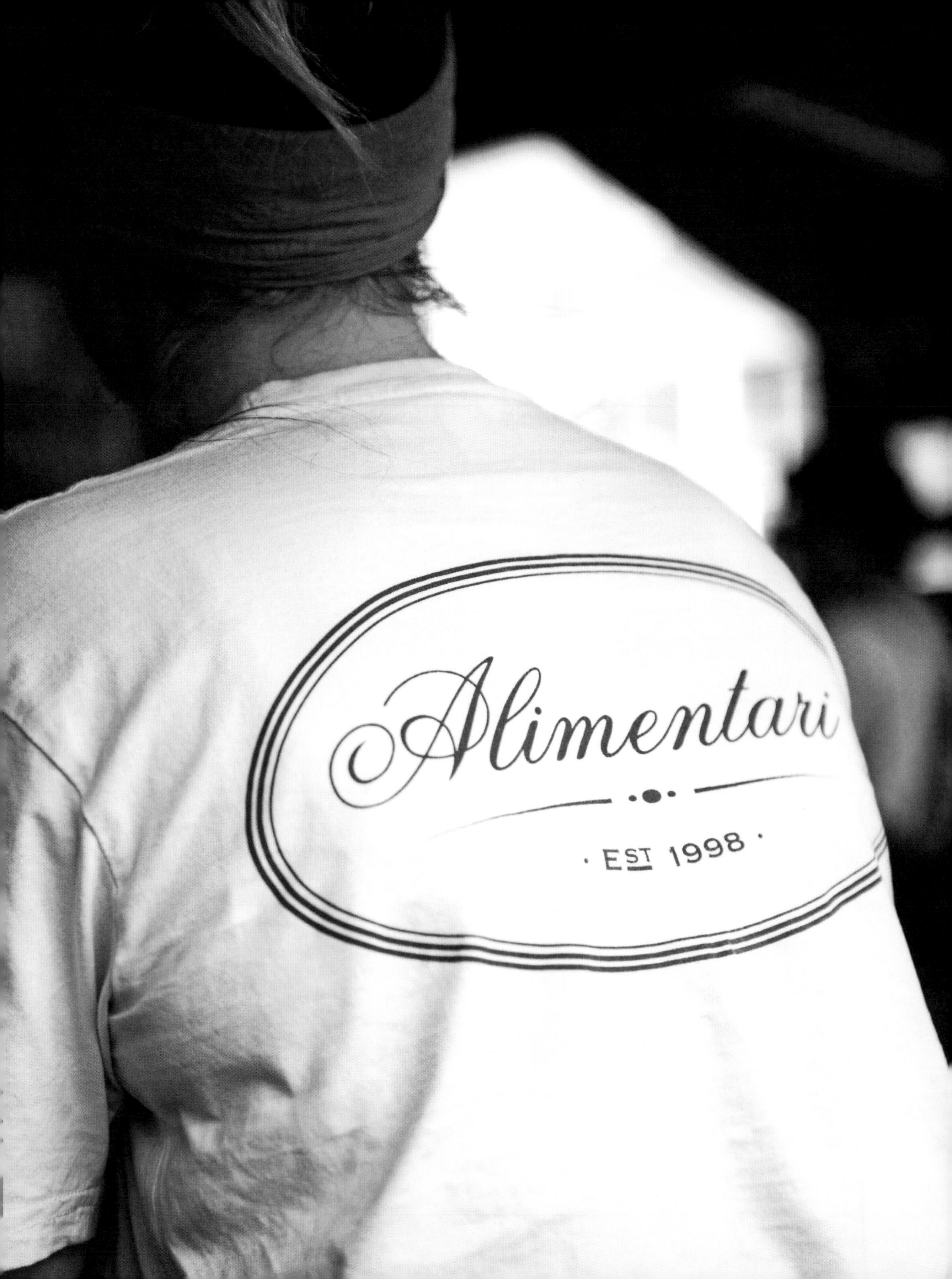
Alimentari
· EST 1998 ·

MORNING

BREAKFAST

BEST

MINI BREAKFAST CIABATTAS

TOMATO BRUSCHETTA

SPANISH TORTILLA OF CONFIT POTATO,
CARAMELISED ONION & THYME

SMOKED SALMON, PERSIAN FETA,
DILL & CHERRY TOMATO TARTS

BEST

The bacon, egg, spinach and tomato ciabatta, or BEST, as it became known, was our first traditional cooked breakfast item. Our original kitchen was incredibly limited (we had a domestic stove from the 1980s with only two electric burners, one of which was broken) so we didn't have the capacity to serve full breakfasts. We wanted to offer bacon and eggs on the go and so the BEST was born. It's still incredibly popular – we wouldn't dare take it off the menu.

4 rashers (slices) kaiserfleisch (or other good smoky bacon)

2 round ciabatta rolls

Aioli (page 180), for spreading

Tomato chutney (page 183), for spreading

1 handful baby spinach leaves

4 slices tomato

4 slices provolone cheese

2 eggs

olive oil, for frying

Heat a frying pan over medium–high heat. Add the kaiserfleisch and fry until cooked to your liking. Remove and drain on paper towel.

Slice the rolls in half and place under a grill (broiler) until lightly toasted.

Spread the bottom halves of the toasted ciabatta with aioli, and the top halves with tomato chutney. Divide the spinach between the rolls, placing on top of the aioli. Top with the tomato and season with pepper. Add the cooked kaiserfleisch and the provolone (if you wish to melt the cheese, place under the grill for 30 seconds).

Meanwhile, heat a little olive oil in a frying pan over medium–high heat. Crack the eggs into the pan and fry until cooked to your liking.

Place the eggs on top of the cheese and season with salt. Cover with the ciabatta tops and you have the perfect breakfast burger.

Makes 4
MINI BREAKFAST CIABATTAS

These were inspired by the little rolls we ate every morning when we were travelling in Spain. They would be piled up on a bar and people would come in and grab one to have with coffee. So many of our customers are rushing in on their way to work and don't have the time or the appetite for a large breakfast – this is the perfect little savoury snack to go.

8 eggs

1 tablespoon milk

¾ tablespoon butter

4 mini ciabatta buns, sliced in half

4 slices prosciutto

Crack the eggs into a medium-sized bowl, add the milk and lightly beat with a fork. Season with salt and pepper.

Melt the butter in a frying pan over medium heat. Before the butter starts to foam, pour in the egg. Stir occasionally until scrambled and cooked to your liking. Divide the scrambled egg among the mini bun bases.

Wipe the frying pan and return to medium heat. Place the prosciutto in the pan and cook until crisp.

Place the prosciutto on top of the eggs and cover with the bun tops.

NOTE: YOU CAN REPLACE THE PROSCIUTTO WITH SLOW-COOKED WINTER GREENS (PAGE 194) FOR A VEGETARIAN OPTION.

TOMATO BRUSCHETTA

This is the first breakfast item we offered at the Brunswick Street store in 1998. The combination of flavours is fresh and simple and includes the pesto we make to sell in the deli. It's still a winner, it's still delicious and still very popular.

Lightly toast the bread under a grill (broiler).

Spread the toast with a generous amount of pesto. Break the ricotta up a little and spoon on top of the pesto. Layer with tomato slices, season with salt and pepper, top with basil leaves and then drizzle with olive oil.

4 slices ciabatta or other good bread

about 2 tablespoons Pesto (page 183)

100 g (3½ oz) fresh ricotta (We love Georgio's ricotta from That's Amore)

2 tomatoes, thickly sliced

6 basil leaves, torn

good extra-virgin olive oil, for drizzling

Serves 8–10

SPANISH TORTILLA OF CONFIT POTATO, CARAMELISED ONION & THYME

When Paul lived in London, he shared a house with three Mexican guys. Because they were all broke, they would often make tortilla for dinner, then eat the leftovers in the morning. It was a revelation to Paul that you could eat tortilla for breakfast! This particular recipe was inspired by a dish Paul used to cook when he worked at Benito's with chef Chris Kerr. Our tortilla is a little unusual as we confit the potatoes and onions in oil first, which really brings out the flavours.

Preheat the oven to160°C (320°F).

Place the potato, onion, garlic and thyme in a medium-sized saucepan and top with the oil. Cook over very low heat for 15–20 minutes, until the potatoes are tender. Strain into a colander set over a large saucepan (to catch the oil) and allow to cool. The strained oil will be quite flavoursome and can be stored in the fridge and used again for frying or roasting.

In a large mixing bowl, combine the eggs, cream and parsley, and season well with salt and pepper. Add the cooled potato mixture and stir to combine.

Heat 2 tablespoons of olive oil in an oven-proof frying pan over medium heat. Pour the potato–egg mixture into the pan and stir gently for 2 minutes. Place the pan in the oven and cook for 15–20 minutes, until set.

Remove from the oven and set aside to cool for 10 minutes. Jiggle the frying pan to ensure that the tortilla will come loose, then, using a plate to cover the top of the frying pan, turn out (you may have to give the pan a bit more of a shake to loosen).

Cut into wedges and serve hot or at room temperature.

1kg (2 lb 3 oz) waxy potatoes (such as desiree), peeled and cut into quarters

2 brown onions, sliced

3 garlic cloves, crushed

3 sprigs thyme

500 ml (17 fl oz/2 cups) olive oil, plus extra for frying

8 eggs

500 ml (17 fl oz/2 cups) pouring (single/light) cream

2 large handfuls flat-leaf (Italian) parsley leaves, finely chopped

Makes 4

SMOKED SALMON,
PERSIAN FETA, DILL
& CHERRY TOMATO TARTS

This recipe was inspired by Rose Bakery in Paris. We wanted something on our menu resembling the tarts and quiches they serve there. Smoked salmon works the best here but you could also use smoked trout, or swap the fish for zucchini (courgette) or mushrooms for a delicious vegetarian version. We sell a lot of these tarts takeaway as they're just as good at room temperature as they are warm.

Preheat the oven to 180°C (350°F). Grease four 8 cm (3¼ in) square baking tins.

Cut or roll out the puff pastry into four 10 cm (4 in) squares. Place the pastry into the prepared tins, pressing down around the centre and edges. Prick the pastry a few times with a fork then cover each tart with an oversized square of baking paper and fill with baking weights, or dry rice or beans. Blind bake for 10 minutes.

In a mixing bowl, whisk together the eggs, cream and parsley until combined. Season with salt and pepper. Remove the tart cases from the oven and set aside the baking paper and weights. Divide the mixture evenly among the tins, top with half of the tomatoes and half of the salmon and bake for 15–20 minutes, until the egg is set and golden.

Allow to cool on a rack for 10 minutes before removing the tarts from the tins. Top with the remaining salmon and tomatoes and the feta, dill and watercress. Drizzle with extra-virgin olive oil and season with salt and pepper.

400 g (14 oz) puff pastry

3 eggs

150 ml (5 fl oz) pouring (single/light) cream

1 handful flat-leaf (Italian) parsley leaves, finely chopped

8 cherry tomatoes, cut in half

200 g (7 oz) smoked salmon, shredded

100 g (3½ oz) Persian feta

dill sprigs, to garnish

watercress, to garnish

extra-virgin olive oil, for drizzling

BRUNCH

SEMOLINA PORRIDGE WITH
RHUBARB COMPOTE & NUTMEG

CORN CAKES WITH GRILLED BACON,
AVOCADO SALSA & POACHED EGGS

HASH BROWNS WITH POACHED EGGS,
SPINACH, BACON & HOLLANDAISE

PERSIAN EGGS

Serves 4

SEMOLINA PORRIDGE WITH RHUBARB COMPOTE & NUTMEG

This came to us through one of our great friends, Theresa Reginato.
T's mother used to make this porridge for her when she was growing up.
She served it with honey but we like it with fruit.

To make the rhubarb compote, combine the sugar with 100 ml (3½ fl oz) of water in a heavy-based saucepan over medium heat and cook for about 5 minutes, until it turns a light golden caramel colour. Add the apple and the marsala. Continue cooking until the caramel has turned back into a liquid. Add the vanilla bean and seeds and the cinnamon stick, and turn the heat to low. Continue cooking for 3 minutes until the apple softens. Add the rhubarb and cook for a further 10 minutes. Remove from the heat, add the raspberries and mix to combine. Transfer to a bowl and set aside to cool.

In a medium-sized saucepan over medium heat, bring the milk and cream to the boil and slowly whisk in the semolina. Continue whisking for about 5 minutes or until thickened.

To serve, divide the porridge between four bowls and spoon the rhubarb compote on top. Sprinkle with a little freshly grated nutmeg.

700 ml (23½ fl oz) milk

300 ml (10 fl oz) pouring (single/light) cream

100 g (3½ oz) fine semolina

freshly grated nutmeg, for sprinkling

RHUBARB COMPOTE

150 g (5½ oz) sugar

2 apples, cored and each cut into 8 wedges

100 ml (3½ fl oz) marsala (make sure it's a good Italian marsala) or orange or apple juice

1 vanilla bean, split and seeds scraped

1 cinnamon stick

4 stalks rhubarb, cut into 5 cm (2 in) lengths

125 g (4½ oz) fresh or frozen raspberries

CORN CAKES WITH GRILLED BACON, AVOCADO SALSA & POACHED EGGS

A classic breakfast dish that we've had on the menu for forever and a day, originally inspired by the corn cakes at Bill's in Sydney. The poached egg is the key to making this dish great – it has to be oozy and runny.

To prepare the corn cakes, sift the flour, baking powder, salt and cayenne pepper into a bowl. In a separate large mixing bowl, combine the egg, milk and sugar. Add the dry ingredients along with the corn kernels, capsicum, chilli, spring onion and herbs and mix until well combined.

To make the salsa, gently combine all of the ingredients in a bowl.

Heat the olive oil in a frying pan over medium heat. Add ¼-cup amounts of the corn cake batter to the pan and cook for 3 minutes on each side or until golden. Remove and set aside to drain on paper towel, then repeat with the remaining batter. You should get eight corn cakes.

In the same pan, fry the bacon until cooked to your liking. Drain on paper towel.

Meanwhile, fill a shallow lidded saucepan or deep frying pan with about 5 cm (2 in) of water. Add the vinegar and bring to the boil over medium–high heat. Turn off the heat and carefully crack the eggs into the water, one at a time. Ensure you are doing this as close to the water surface as possible so as to contain the egg. Place the lid on the pan and leave the eggs to poach for 2–3 minutes. The eggs are cooked when the whites are solid.

Stack two corn cakes on each plate and top with a poached egg. Serve with the bacon and salsa on the side.

2 tablespoons olive oil

8 rashers (slices) bacon

1 teaspoon vinegar

4 eggs

CORN CAKES

250 g (9 oz/1⅔ cup) cup plain (all-purpose) flour

1 teaspoon baking powder

1 teaspoon salt

1 teaspoon cayenne pepper

3 eggs, lightly beaten

180 ml (6 fl oz) milk

1 tablespoon sugar

3 cups corn kernels (about 4 cobs)

½ red capsicum (bell pepper), diced

1 long red chilli, deseeded and chopped

3–4 spring onions (scallions), finely sliced

1 handful coriander (cilantro) leaves, chopped

1 handful flat-leaf (Italian) parsley, chopped

AVOCADO SALSA

2 avocadoes, flesh finely diced

juice of 1 lime

2 handfuls coriander (cilantro) leaves, finely chopped

1 tomato, diced

¼ red onion, finely diced

4 drops Tobasco sauce

1 tablespoon extra-virgin olive oil

HASH BROWNS WITH POACHED EGGS, SPINACH, BACON & HOLLANDAISE

This dish obviously shares its origins with the classic Eggs Benedict but one of our chefs, Mel Musu, came up with the great idea of replacing the muffin with a hash brown. The hash browns are a bit time-consuming as there are a few steps involved, but the end result is definitely worth the extra time.

To prepare the hash browns, place the potatoes in a large saucepan of cold salted water and bring to the boil. Reduce to a simmer and cook for 5 minutes, then drain in a colander. Place the potatoes on a tray and refrigerate for at least 2 hours (but ideally until completely cold). Coarsely grate the cooled potatoes and transfer to a mixing bowl. Add the onion, egg, breadcrumbs and seasoning and stir to combine. Form into four 5 cm (2 in) round patties, about 1.5 cm (½ in) thick.

Heat the oil in a deep-fryer, or in a medium-sized saucepan over high heat, until it reaches 175°C (345°F) or until a cube of bread dropped into the oil turns brown in 20 seconds. Fry the hash browns, two at a time, for 3 minutes or until crisp and golden. Drain on paper towel and season with salt.

Meanwhile, in a frying pan over medium–low heat, melt the butter with the olive oil and sauté the spinach until just wilted. Set aside. In the same pan, fry the bacon until cooked to your liking.

Meanwhile, fill a shallow lidded saucepan or deep frying pan with about 5 cm (2 in) of water. Add the vinegar and bring to the boil over medium–high heat. Turn off the heat and carefully crack the eggs into the water, one at a time. Ensure you are doing this as close to the water surface as possible so as to contain the egg. Place the lid on the pan and leave the eggs to poach for 2–3 minutes. The eggs are cooked when the whites are solid.

To serve, divide the hash browns among four plates. Place the spinach and bacon alongside, top with a poached egg and drizzle with hollandaise sauce.

canola or sunflower oil for deep-frying

½ tablespoon butter

1 teaspoon olive oil

2 cups baby spinach leaves

8 rashers (slices) bacon

1 teaspoon vinegar

4 eggs

1 quantity Hollandaise sauce (page 184)

HASH BROWNS

1 kg (2 lb 3 oz) potatoes, peeled

2 brown onions, finely diced

2 eggs, lightly beaten

100 g (3½ oz/1 cup) dry breadcrumbs

1 teaspoon celery salt

1 teaspoon freshly ground black pepper

1 teaspoon salt

Serves 2
PERSIAN EGGS

We have a few customers who come in regularly just for this breakfast. We once tried taking it off the menu for a change. Big mistake! Sorry, Trish, it won't happen again.

In a mixing bowl, combine the eggs and cream and season with salt and pepper.

Melt the butter or ghee in a medium-sized frying pan over medium heat. Add the egg mixture and stir gently until the egg starts to set. Add the spinach and stir until it just begins to wilt.

Divide the eggs between two plates and sprinkle with feta and dukkah. Serve with fresh Lebanese flatbread or toast.

3 eggs

1 tablespoon pouring (single/light) cream

1 teaspoon butter or ghee

1 tablespoon Persian feta

1 tablespoon Dukkah (page 182)

small handful baby spinach leaves

2 pieces fresh Lebanese flatbread or buttered wholegrain toast

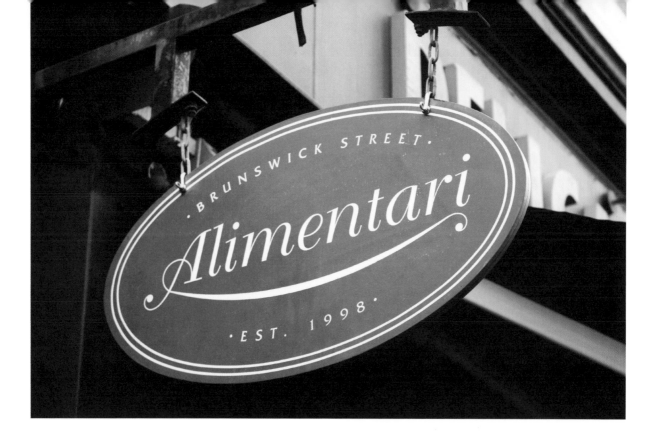

MIDDAY

TAKEAWAYS

MEATBALL WRAP

CHICKEN SCHNITZEL WRAP

BUFFALO MOZZARELLA, PROSCIUTTO,
BASIL & TOMATO PIADINA

HALOUMI PIES

SPINACH PIES

Serves 2
MEATBALL
WRAP

Arguably, this is Alimentari's signature sandwich. Dolores and I came up with this incredible morsel after a big night out at the club Honky Tonks. It's a perfect fusion of our Italian and Lebanese backgrounds and, most importantly, the best hangover cure around. This recipe has been borrowed, adapted, even outright stolen, but in my humble opinion, our original is by far the best.

Aioli (page 180), for spreading

2 pieces Lebanese flatbread

1 large handful baby spinach leaves

6 Pork & veal meatballs (page 96)

1 lemon, cut in half

4 slices cheddar cheese

Preheat a flat sandwich press (optional).

Spread the aioli evenly over the bread. Top with a row of baby spinach leaves.

Place the meatballs along the rows of spinach and gently squash them. Squeeze with lemon juice, season to taste and crumble the cheese over the meatballs.

Fold the bread over at each end of the row of filling. Bring one side over the top and fold and roll, pressing down slightly to flatten, until you have a nice tight wrap.

If desired, place in a sandwich press for 8–10 mins (5 mins if your meatballs are already hot). If you don't have a sandwich press, simply add your meatballs hot, wrap and eat untoasted.

Serves 2

CHICKEN SCHNITZEL WRAP

I'm sure some customers wouldn't mind if all we sold were chicken schnitzel wraps all day long. People cross town for these and get upset when we sell out (which we always do).

Preheat a flat sandwich press (optional).

Spread the aioli evenly over the bread. Top with a row of lettuce and tomato. Season with pepper then crumble the cheese over the top.

Slice the chicken diagonally and place along the cheese. Squeeze with lemon juice and top with cucumber. Season with salt.

Fold the bread over at each end of the row of filling. Bring one side over the top and fold and roll, pressing down slightly to flatten, until you have a nice tight wrap.

If desired, place in a sandwich press for 5 minutes. If you don't have a sandwich press, warm the chicken first and eat untoasted.

2 pieces Lebanese flatbread

Aioli (page 180), for spreading

a few leaves cos (romaine) lettuce, coarsely chopped

1 tomato, sliced

4 slices cheddar cheese

2 Chicken schnitzels (page 100)

1 lemon, cut in half

½ Lebanese cucumber, sliced

Sorry, but lard is the secret to piadina. It kind of holds everything together and makes it crispy. I adore piadinas. You can have them as a snack – it's like a calzone in some ways but really thin. Best of all they're very achievable at home because the dough is easy to work with. You just pan fry the dough, put the filling in and off you go.

To make the dough, mix the dry ingredients together by hand in a large mixing bowl. Add the melted lard or butter and gently combine. Gradually add enough of the water to form a dough. Cover the bowl with plastic wrap and leave in a warm place to rest for 30 minutes.

Divide the dough into four portions of about 90 g (3 oz) each. Roll out into 20 cm (8 in) rounds.

Heat a little olive oil in a frying pan over high heat. Fry each piadina for a few minutes on each side, or until lightly coloured.

Top one half of each piadina with slices of mozzarella, prosciutto, tomato and basil. Fold over and enjoy fresh or toasted in a flat sandwich press.

olive oil, for frying

1 x 125 g (4½ oz) ball fresh buffalo mozzarella, sliced

8 slices prosciutto

2 tomatoes, sliced

1 handful basil leaves

PIADINA DOUGH

185 g (6½ oz/1¼ cups) plain (all-purpose) flour

¼ teaspoon bicarbonate of soda (baking soda)

pinch of salt

25 g (1 oz) lard or butter, melted

about 90 ml (3 fl oz) warm water

Makes 10–12 pies
HALOUMI PIES

All the pies we make are best eaten straight out of the oven, so if we have any haloumi pies left over we don't sell them the next day. But they're too good to waste, so sometimes we stuff them with meatballs and spinach and then toast them, to make crazy Lebanese-Italian fusion snacks.

Preheat the oven to 260°C (500°F) or the highest temperature it will go. Grease two large baking trays.

Divide the pie dough in half and work with one piece at a time. Roll out onto a well-floured work surface into a rectangle about 3 mm (⅛ in) thick. Cut into 10–12 circles using a 12 cm (4¾ in) cutter. Collect the offcuts and roll out again to use up all of the dough.

Place 2 tablespoons of the haloumi onto one half of each piece of dough. Fold the pastry over to form a semi-circle, then press lightly to push out air and seal the edge. Starting at one end, make a series of small folds to crimp the edge (see photos on the following pages).

Place the pies onto the prepared baking trays and bake for 20 minutes or until golden.

Allow to cool for a few minutes before serving with tomato chutney and a green salad (if desired).

1 quantity Lebanese pie dough (page 188)

1 kg (2 lb 3 oz) haloumi, coarsely grated

Tomato chutney (page 183), to serve (optional)

green salad, to serve (optional)

Makes 10–12 pies

SPINACH PIES

From day one of Brunswick Street Alimentari, my mum was making pies for us from home every morning, seven days a week, for about ten years. She'd make about twenty spinach pies, twenty Haloumi pies and twenty Sambusic (pages 45 and 142) – sixty pies a day delivered hot to us every morning. This was one of the things that first put the deli on the map – a quick, tasty and cheap snack that everybody loved.

1 bunch (about 250 g/9 oz) spinach, washed, drained and roughly chopped

1 large onion, diced

1 teaspoon Baharat (page 182)

1 teaspoon salt

2 tablespoons lemon juice

2 tablespoons olive oil

1 quantity Lebanese pie dough (page 188)

Preheat the oven to 260°C (500°F) or the highest temperature it will go. Grease two large baking trays.

Squeeze any excess moisture from the spinach and place into a bowl. Add the onion, baharat, salt, lemon juice and olive oil, and toss to combine well.

Divide the pie dough in half and work with one piece at a time. Roll out onto a well-floured work surface into a rectangle about 3 mm (⅛ in) thick. Cut out circles using a 12 cm (4¾ in) cutter. Collect the offcuts and roll out again to use up all of the dough. You should get 10–12 circles.

Spoon 2 tablespoons of the spinach mixture into the centre of each dough circle. Bring up the dough into three sides and press the edges together to form a pyramid.

Place the pies onto the prepared baking trays and bake for 20 minutes or until golden.

SALADS

BLOOD ORANGE & FENNEL SALAD WITH
CURRANTS & AGRO DOLCE DRESSING

RAW VEGETABLE SALAD WITH
HONEY DRESSING

CHARGRILLED VEGETABLE SALAD WITH
COUSCOUS, SPICED YOGHURT & ALMONDS

GRILLED FIGS WITH BURRATA,
ROASTED WALNUTS & PROSCIUTTO

GREEN SESAME SALAD

BAHARAT-SPICED FRENCH BEANS
WITH PUY LENTILS & TOMATO

ROASTED BROCCOLI, SESAME & TOFU
WITH GINGER DRESSING

LEBANESE CUCUMBER & TOMATO SALAD
WITH SHANKLISH & RED ONION

RED QUINOA, WITLOF, WALNUT, CHERRY
TOMATO & POMEGRANATE SALAD

SAFFRON RICE WITH CHICKPEAS,
LENTILS & BAHARAT

PICKLED BEETROOT SALAD WITH
WALNUTS, HAZELNUTS & SHANKLISH

CAULIFLOWER & CHICKPEA SALAD WITH
ALMONDS, FRIED ONION & SULTANAS

WATERMELON WITH HALOUMI,
PINE NUTS, SUMAC & MINT

RED SALAD

FENNEL, PEAR, KOHLRABI
& WATERCRESS SALAD

BEETROOT, LENTIL
& RICOTTA SALATA

VERMICELLI NOODLE SALAD WITH
THAI CHILLI DRESSING

GRILLED ZUCCHINI WITH COUSCOUS,
SMOKED EGGPLANT & PANGRITATA

RISONI SALAD WITH ASPARAGUS,
ZUCCHINI, LEMON & RICOTTA

AVOCADO, CHERRY TOMATO
& DUKKAH SALAD

FARRO, PERSIAN FETA
& ALMOND SALAD

ROASTED PUMPKIN, ROCKET,
BALSAMIC ONION & PARMESAN

Serves 4–6 as a starter or light meal

BLOOD ORANGE & FENNEL SALAD WITH CURRANTS & AGRO DOLCE DRESSING

I'm a massive fan of fennel, I love blood orange and I really like the agro dolce flavours: sweet, sour and bitter – so this salad is made up of a lot of my favourite things. If blood oranges are out of season, navel oranges are a fine substitute. We also sometimes use apples or stone fruit, but citrus is lighter and great for summer.

Remove the white pith from the oranges using a small sharp knife. Working over a bowl to catch the juice, cut between each membrane to remove the segments. Squeeze out the remaining juice from the core and reserve for the dressing.

To make the dressing, heat a splash of oil in a small saucepan over low heat. Add the onion and gently cook until golden brown. Add the sugar and the vinegars, and continue cooking until the sugar is dissolved and the liquid has reduced by a third. Remove from the heat and set aside to cool. Once cooled, strain out the onions, whisk in the reserved orange juice and the olive oil and season to taste.

Give all of the salad leaves a good wash and allow to dry in a colander.

Gently fold all of the salad ingredients together with the dressing in a large salad bowl. Season with salt and pepper.

~~~~~~~~

NOTE: ROCKET (ARUGULA) IS A GOOD SUBSTITUTE IF CHICORY (ENDIVE) IS UNAVAILABLE.

3 blood oranges, peeled

2 red witlof (chicory/Belgian endive), core removed and leaves separated

1 head radicchio, leaves separated and broken

1 bunch chicory (endive), stems and leaves cut into 3 cm (1¼ in) pieces

2 fennel bulbs, fronds chopped and bulbs finely sliced on a mandoline

100 g (3½ oz) currants, soaked for 30 minutes in enough water to cover

1 bunch dill, picked

AGRO DOLCE DRESSING

oil, for frying

1 red onion, thinly sliced

50 g (1¾ oz) caster sugar

75 ml (2½ fl oz) aged red-wine vinegar

75 ml (2½ fl oz) balsamic vinegar

100 ml (3½ fl oz) olive oil

Serves 4–6 as a starter or light meal

RAW VEGETABLE SALAD WITH HONEY DRESSING

Over the past five years, more and more people are looking for healthy, vegetarian and gluten-free dishes. This salad is all those things. It's also really light and one of our best-sellers.

Preheat the oven to 150°C (300°F).

Peel away and discard the two outer layers of leaves on the brussels sprouts (you only want to use the tender centre leaves). Finely slice using a mandoline or a food processor with a cutting attachment on the lowest setting.

Cut the remaining vegetables and apple into matchsticks using a julienne peeler or mandoline attachment. Cut the beetroot last and keep separate to avoid turning everything purple.

Spread the pepitas and sunflower seeds onto a baking tray and toast in the oven for 5 minutes or until golden brown.

To make the dressing, combine the honey, lemon juice and sherry vinegar in a small bowl. Slowly whisk in the olive oil and season to taste.

To assemble the salad, combine all of the vegetables except the beetroot with the dressing in a salad bowl. Very gently fold the beetroot through, sprinkle the nigella seeds over and top with the herbs.

100 g (3½ oz) brussels sprouts

200 g (7 oz) carrots, peeled

200 g (7 oz) zucchini (courgettes)

2 granny smith apples, cored

100 g (3½ oz) snow peas

100 g (3½ oz) beetroot (beets)

100 g (3½ oz) bean sprouts

50 g (1¾ oz) pepitas (pumpkin seeds)

50 g (1¾ oz) sunflower seeds

50 g (1¾ oz) nigella seeds

½ bunch coriander (cilantro), leaves picked

½ bunch flat-leaf (Italian) parsley, leaves picked

HONEY DRESSING

1 tablespoon honey

200 ml (7 fl oz) lemon juice

60 ml (2 fl oz/¼ cup) sherry vinegar

200 ml (7 fl oz) olive oil

Serves 4–6 as a starter or light meal
CHARGRILLED VEGETABLE SALAD WITH COUSCOUS, SPICED YOGHURT & ALMONDS

Chargrilling is a great way to put extra flavour into vegetables. It adds an extra layer of depth and smokiness. You can serve this salad as a starter by smearing Baba ghanooj (page 109) across the plate and piling the vegetables on top.

Preheat the oven to 180°C (350°F).

To make the dressing, place all of the ingredients in a bowl and whisk to combine.

Place the capsicums on a baking tray and roast for 30 minutes or until the skin begins to blister. Remove from the oven and place in a bowl. Cover with plastic wrap and allow to cool. Once cold peel the skins from the peppers and slice the flesh.

In a saucepan, combine the olive oil and salt with 500 ml (17 fl oz/2 cups) of water and bring to the boil. Place the couscous in a large heatproof bowl. Pour the boiling water over, cover with plastic wrap and leave to sit for 10 minutes to absorb. Once cool, use a fork to separate the couscous.

Place the ghee in a shallow frying pan over low heat. When melted, add the almonds and cook until golden. This happens quite quickly so make sure you keep your eye on the ball while tossing the almonds around. Drain on paper towel.

Combine the eggplant, zucchini and fennel in a bowl. Season with salt and pepper, drizzle with olive oil and mix to coat. Heat an oiled chargrill pan or heavy-based frying pan to very hot over high heat. Grill the vegetables on both sides until well coloured. Transfer to a baking tray and bake for 10 minutes or until soft. Meanwhile, combine the onion and asparagus in a bowl with a drizzle of oil. Grill until well coloured.

To serve, combine the vegetables with the couscous and parsley in a bowl. Season well, add half the yoghurt dressing and combine carefully. Spread onto a serving plate, sprinkle with the almonds and drizzle with a little extra-virgin olive oil and the remaining dressing.

3 red capsicums (bell peppers)

50 ml (1¾ fl oz) olive oil, plus extra for drizzling

1 tablespoon salt

500 g (1 lb 2 oz) pearl (Israeli) couscous

1½ tablespoons ghee

150 g (5½ oz) slivered almonds

2 eggplants (aubergines), thickly sliced

4 zucchini (courgettes), thickly sliced

2 fennel bulbs, thickly sliced

2 red onions, thickly sliced

1 bunch asparagus, trimmed and cut into bite-sized pieces

½ bunch flat-leaf (Italian) parsley, leaves finely chopped

extra-virgin olive oil, for drizzling

SPICED YOGHURT DRESSING

250 g (9 oz/1 cup) Greek-style yoghurt

100 ml (3½ fl oz) lemon juice

1 teaspoon salt

1 teaspoon freshly ground pepper

1 garlic clove, crushed

1 teaspoon chilli flakes

1 teaspoon ground cumin

1 handful coriander (cilantro) leaves, chopped

Serves 4–6 as a starter or light meal
GRILLED FIGS WITH BURRATA, ROASTED WALNUTS & PROSCIUTTO

We love burrata and we particularly love the burrata that we get from Giorgio Linguanti from La Latteria, our local fromagerie. And creamy cheese paired with figs is hard to beat. My parents have a massive fig tree in their backyard and every year it's, 'Quick, come and pick the figs before the birds get them.' And so we end up with an abundance, which is not a bad problem to have.

Preheat the oven to 140°C (275°F). Line a tray with baking paper.

In a small saucepan over low heat, melt the butter together with the brown sugar. Add the walnuts and stir well to coat. Pour the nuts onto the prepared tray and bake for 15 minutes or until well toasted (be careful as the nuts can burn easily). Set aside to cool.

Heat an oiled chargrill pan or heavy-based frying pan to very hot over high heat. Sprinkle a little sugar over the cut sides of the figs, then grill, cut side down for about 30 seconds.

To assemble, arrange the grilled figs on a platter with the prosciutto, rocket and walnuts. Tear the burrata over the top of the salad then drizzle with the balsamic and olive oil. Season well with salt and pepper.

~~~~~~~~~

NOTE: BURRATA IS A COW'S MILK CHEESE ORIGINALLY FROM MURGIA IN SOUTHERN ITALY. IT HAS AN OUTER SHELL MADE FROM MOZZARELLA AND A SOFT CENTRE MADE FROM A MIX OF MOZZARELLA AND CREAM. BURRATA IS AVAILABLE FROM GOOD ITALIAN DELIS, BUT YOU CAN SUBSTITUTE FRESH BUFFALO MOZZARELLA IF UNAVAILABLE.

100 g (3½ oz) butter

100 g (3½ oz/½ cup) brown sugar

25 g (1 oz/¼ cup) walnuts

sugar, for sprinkling

8 figs, cut in half

1 burrata (see note)

8 prosciutto slices

1 large handful rocket (arugula) leaves

2 tablespoons balsamic vinegar

2 tablespoons extra-virgin olive oil

Serves 4–6 as a starter or light meal
GREEN SESAME SALAD

This is one of the newer salads on our menu and was inspired by Paul's recent trip to California. He discovered a chain of salad restaurants around LA called Lemonade, which he thinks are the best salad places he's ever been to – cheap, fresh and delicious. Just like this salad really.

To make the dressing, place all of the ingredients in a small bowl and whisk to combine.

Prepare an ice bath by filling a large bowl with water and adding ice cubes.

Bring a large saucepan of salted water to the boil and add the peas, green beans and edamame. Cook for 2 minutes then drain and refresh in the ice bath. Transfer to a salad bowl.

To assemble the salad, place the all the remaining ingredients into the salad bowl with the blanched peas and beans, drizzle the dressing over and toss well to coat. Season to taste with salt and pepper.

200 g (7 oz) sugar-snap peas, trimmed and cut in half diagonally

200 g (7 oz) snow peas, trimmed and cut in half diagonally

150 g (5½ oz) green beans, trimmed and cut in half diagonally

500 g (1 lb 2 oz) podded edamame

150 g (5½ oz) fresh mung beans

3 shallots, finely sliced

1 handful snow pea tendrils

1 bunch coriander (cilantro), leaves picked and finely chopped

1 tablespoon sesame seeds

1 tablespoon black sesame seeds

SESAME DRESSING

125 ml (4 fl oz/½ cup) rice vinegar

1 garlic clove, crushed

1 tablespoon dijon mustard

125 ml (4 fl oz/½ cup) soy sauce

125 ml (4 fl oz/½ cup) vegetable oil

2 tablespoons sesame oil

BAHARAT-SPICED FRENCH BEANS WITH PUY LENTILS & TOMATO

This is my mum's recipe, her version of a classic Lebanese green bean dish. You can eat it hot or at room temperature (I think it's best at the latter). It's great as part of a mezze but you can also have it as a main with yoghurt and Lebanese bread.

Heat the oil in a large saucepan with a well-fitting lid over medium–low heat. Add the onions and cook for 3 minutes, or until they begin to soften without colouring. Stir in the garlic, cover with the lid and cook for 3 minutes.

Turn the heat to the lowest setting. Add the beans and the stock or water, replace the lid and cook for 30 minutes, stirring every 10 minutes or so.

Add the tomato paste, diced tomatoes, baharat and salt, and continue to cook for a further 30 minutes. The beans will be very soft and dark green and the tomato reduced.

Meanwhile, bring a saucepan of water to the boil. Add the lentils and cook over low heat for 20 minutes or until tender. Drain.

While the lentils are still warm, combine with the beans and season to taste. Drizzle with some good extra-virgin olive oil and allow to cool to room temperature before serving.

150 ml (5 fl oz) olive oil

2 brown onions, finely sliced

3 garlic cloves, finely chopped

1 kg (2 lb 3 oz) green beans, trimmed

250 ml (8½ fl oz/1 cup) vegetable stock or water

1 tablespoon tomato paste

1 × 400 g (14 oz) tin diced tomatoes

3 tablespoons Baharat (page 182)

1 tablespoon salt

300 g (10½ oz) puy lentils, rinsed

extra-virgin olive oil, for drizzling

Serves 4–6 as a starter or light meal

ROASTED BROCCOLI, SESAME & TOFU WITH GINGER DRESSING

Broccoli salads are always our most popular. Put broccoli with anything and it will walk out the door. Raw, blanched, braised, anything – broccoli sells.

Preheat the oven to 200°C (400°F). Line a baking tray with baking paper.

Place the broccoli in a large bowl and coat with the olive oil and season well with salt and pepper. Spread out on the prepared tray and bake for around 12 minutes or until browned. Remove and set aside to cool.

Prepare an ice bath by filling a large bowl with water and adding ice cubes.

Bring a large saucepan of salted water to the boil and cook the snow peas and edamame for 1 minute. Drain and refresh in the ice bath. Transfer to a salad bowl.

To make the ginger dressing, whisk all the ingredients together in a small bowl with 60 ml (2 fl oz/¼ cup) of water. Season to taste.

Add the cooled broccoli to the salad bowl, along with the remaining ingredients, except the tofu. Pour the dressing over, toss well to combine, then scatter the tofu over the top.

2 heads broccoli (about 1 kg/ 2 lb 3 oz), divided into florets

200 ml (7 fl oz) olive oil

100 g (3½ oz) snow peas, trimmed and cut in half diagonally

250 g (9 oz) podded edamame

250 g (9 oz) bean sprouts

3 teaspoons nigella seeds

2–3 tablespoons sesame seeds

1 bunch spring onions (scallions), trimmed and finely sliced

2 avocadoes, flesh roughly crushed

250 g (9 oz) firm tofu, crumbled

GINGER DRESSING

3 tablespoons finely chopped fresh ginger

2 cloves garlic, crushed

3 tablespoons honey

2 tablespoons miso paste

125 ml (4 fl oz/½ cup) soy sauce

125 ml (4 fl oz/½ cup) rice wine

125 ml (4 fl oz/½ cup) olive oil

Serves 4–6 as a starter or light meal
LEBANESE CUCUMBER & TOMATO SALAD WITH SHANKLISH & RED ONION

This is a version of a traditional fattoush salad that we always have around in some form or another. It's a classic combination of flavours and includes shanklish, one of our favourite things. Shanklish is salty like feta but has more flavour because it's often rolled in chilli or za'atar. It can be a bit much for some people so we've toned it down a bit here – when my mum makes it the shanklish is in the same proportions as the tomatoes, cucumbers and onion.

Preheat the oven to 150°C (300°F). Lightly grease a baking tray.

Place the flatbread onto the prepared tray, sprinkle with salt and drizzle with olive oil. Bake for 10-15 minutes or until golden. Set aside to cool.

Either on one large platter or on individual plates, arrange the tomatoes, ensuring that you have a good mix of colours and sizes, and the onion, cucumber, radish and toasted flatbread. Crumble the shanklish over, sprinkle with the chilli, sumac, mint and spring onion, then drizzle with a good amount of extra-virgin olive oil. Season well with salt and pepper.

~~~~~~~~~

NOTE: FOR THIS SALAD I LIKE TO USE A MIX OF TOMATO VARIETIES SUCH AS GREEN TOMATOES, SMALL YELLOW TOMATOES, TIGER TOMATOES, CHERRY TOMATOES AND TEARDROP TOMATOES.

1 piece Lebanese flatbread, torn into bite-sized pieces

olive oil, for drizzling

300 g (10½ oz) mixed tomatoes (see note), cored and cut into slices or wedges

1 red onion, finely sliced

6 Lebanese cucumbers, cut into ribbons with a peeler

4 radishes, finely sliced

250 g (9 oz) shanklish (see note page 71), crumbled

1 long red chilli, diced

sumac, for sprinkling

1 bunch mint, leaves shredded

½ bunch spring onions (scallions), finely sliced

extra-virgin olive oil, for drizzling

Serves 4–6 as a starter or light meal
RED QUINOA, WITLOF, WALNUT, CHERRY TOMATO & POMEGRANATE SALAD

This salad is one from our menu of healthier salads. The combination of textures and flavours is beautiful. And so good for you!

Preheat the oven to 150°C (300°F).

Spread the walnuts on a baking tray and toast in the oven for 12 minutes, until golden.

Place the quinoa in a saucepan with 1 litre (34 fl oz/4 cups) of water and a pinch of salt. Cover, bring to the boil, then turn down the heat and simmer for 15 minutes, or until the quinoa is tender and the water has been absorbed. Spread onto a tray to cool.

To make the dressing, place all of the ingredients in a small bowl and whisk to combine.

To serve, combine the ingredients in a salad bowl with the dressing. Season well with salt and pepper, and garnish with a sprinkling of sumac.

~~~~~~

NOTE: TO REMOVE POMEGRANATE SEEDS, CUT THE POMEGRANATE IN HALF AND, USING A WOODEN SPOON, SMACK THE SKIN SIDE OF THE POMEGRANATE OVER A BOWL TO CATCH THE SEEDS AS THEY FALL OUT.

100 g (3½ oz/1 cup) walnuts

500 g (1 lb 2 oz) red quinoa

2 red witlof (chicory/Belgian endive), leaves separated

1 red onion, finely sliced

5 radishes, finely sliced on a mandoline

½ red cabbage, finely shredded

1 radicchio, leaves shredded

250 g (9 oz) cherry tomatoes, cut in half

seeds from 2 pomegranates (see note)

sumac, to garnish

DRESSING

100 ml (3½ fl oz) pomegranate molasses

50 ml (1¾ fl oz) red-wine vinegar

100 ml (3½ fl oz) olive oil

1 tablespoon dijon mustard

SAFFRON RICE WITH CHICKPEAS, LENTILS & BAHARAT

Serves 4–6 as a starter or light meal

This is a version of my mum's recipe for mjadra. It's a dish that Dolores and I used to cook all the time and was one of the first Lebanese recipes that she mastered. You can eat it warm, you can eat it cold, you can eat it the next day and it's just as good every time.

Melt the butter in a heavy-based saucepan with a well-fitting lid over low heat. Add the saffron and the rice and stir to coat well. Add the chicken stock and bay leaves, bring to the boil then turn the heat down as low as it will go. Cover and cook for 12–15 minutes until the stock has been absorbed. Remove from the heat and leave to cool for 10 minutes before fluffing the rice with a fork. Spread onto a tray to cool completely.

Meanwhile, bring a large saucepan of water to the boil, add the lentils then reduce the heat to a simmer and cook for 15–20 minutes or until tender. Drain and set aside to cool.

Heat the oil in a medium-sized frying pan over high heat, then add the shallots and fry until crisp and golden brown. Remove and set aside to drain on paper towel.

To make the dressing, combine the lemon juice and baharat in a small bowl. Slowly whisk in the oil and season to taste.

To serve, combine all of the ingredients except the shallots in a large salad bowl and toss with the dressing. Top with the fried shallots.

~~~~~~~~

NOTE: TO COOK CHICKPEAS, START THE NIGHT BEFORE BY SOAKING 125 G (4½ OZ) DRIED CHICKPEAS IN COLD WATER. THE NEXT DAY, DRAIN THEN RINSE THE CHICKPEAS AND PLACE IN A LARGE SAUCEPAN. COVER WITH FRESH WATER AND BRING TO THE BOIL. REDUCE THE HEAT AND COOK FOR 1½ HOURS OR UNTIL TENDER. DRAIN INTO A COLANDER AND TOSS IN A SPLASH OF GOOD OLIVE OIL.

50 g (1¾ oz) butter

1 pinch saffron

200 g (7 oz/1 cup) basmati rice

500 ml (17 fl oz/2 cups) chicken stock

2 fresh bay leaves

150 g (5½ oz) brown lentils

200 ml (7 fl oz) vegetable oil

6 shallots, thinly sliced

200 g (7 oz) cooked (see note) or drained tinned chickpeas

1 bunch coriander (cilantro), leaves picked

1 bunch flat-leaf (Italian) parsley, leaves picked

1 bunch mint, leaves torn

BAHARAT DRESSING

150 ml (5 fl oz) lemon juice

1 tablespoon Baharat (page 182)

100 ml (3½ fl oz) olive oil

Serves 4–6 as a starter or light meal
PICKLED BEETROOT SALAD WITH WALNUTS, HAZELNUTS & SHANKLISH

Beetroot (beets) are always popular and this salad is a ripper with all of its soft, crunchy, salty flavours. It has a bit of everything. We pickle the beetroot in red-wine vinegar and sugar, which adds another dimension to it.

Place the beetroot in a large saucepan with the vinegar, sugar, cinnamon and enough water to cover. Bring to the boil, then reduce the heat to low and cook for 1–1½ hours until tender enough for a knife to pierce the flesh without resistance. Drain and set aside to cool. When cool enough to handle, peel the beetroot and cut into 2 cm (¾ in) cubes. (Make sure you wear kitchen gloves for this.) Transfer to a salad bowl.

Meanwhile, preheat the oven to 150°C (300°F). Line a baking tray with baking paper.

Spread the nuts and seeds onto the prepared tray and toast in the oven for 12 minutes, or until golden.

To assemble the salad, coat the beetroot with the olive oil, place on a plate with the remaining ingredients and scatter the toasted nuts and seeds over. Toss gently and season well with salt and pepper.

~~~~~~~~~

NOTE: SHANKLISH IS A DELICATE CRUMBLY CHEESE OFTEN ROLLED IN THYME, ZA'ATAR AND CHILLI. AVAILABLE FROM MIDDLE EASTERN GROCERS. YOU CAN SUBSTITUTE PERSIAN FETA IF UNAVAILABLE.

800 g (1 lb 12 oz) beetroot (beets)

500 ml (17 fl oz/2 cups) red-wine vinegar

200 g (7 oz) caster sugar

2 cinnamon sticks

150 g (5½ oz/1½ cups) walnuts

100 g (3½ oz/¾ cup) hazelnuts

100 g (3½ oz/¾ cup) pepitas (pumpkin seeds)

100 g (3½ oz) sunflower seeds

150 ml (5 fl oz) extra-virgin olive oil

½ bunch dill, roughly chopped

1 small handful mint, roughly chopped

2 handfuls baby spinach leaves, torn

250 g (9 oz) shanklish, crumbled (see note)

Serves 4–6 as a starter or light meal

CAULIFLOWER & CHICKPEA SALAD WITH ALMONDS, FRIED ONION & SULTANAS

This is inspired by a classic Lebanese fried cauliflower dish that I've primarily eaten as a sandwich – fried cauliflower and houmus rolled up in flatbread. We dress the salad with tahini but you could also use houmous. I love this with a side of fresh Lebanese bread.

Preheat the oven to 150°C (300°F). Lightly grease a baking tray.

Fill a small saucepan about 2 cm (¾ in) full with oil and heat until it just starts to shimmer. Add the cauliflower and fry until golden brown. Remove and drain on paper towel. Then add the onions and cook until crisp and lightly golden. Remove and drain.

Spread the flatbread onto the prepared tray, sprinkle with salt and drizzle with olive oil. Bake for 10-15 minutes or until golden. Set aside to cool.

Place the ghee in a shallow frying pan over low heat. When melted, add the almonds and cook until golden. This happens quite quickly so make sure you keep your eye on the ball while tossing the almonds around. Drain on paper towel.

To make the dressing, place all of the ingredients in a small bowl and whisk to combine.

To serve, fold the chickpeas, sultanas, almonds and cauliflower together in a large salad bowl. Add the coriander, parsley and basil, top with the fried onion and drizzle the tahini dressing over. Finally, gently fold in the toasted flatbread.

~~~~~~~~~~

NOTE: TO COOK CHICKPEAS, START THE NIGHT BEFORE BY SOAKING 125 G (4½ OZ) DRIED CHICKPEAS IN COLD WATER. THE NEXT DAY, DRAIN THEN RINSE THE CHICKPEAS AND PLACE IN A LARGE SAUCEPAN. COVER WITH FRESH WATER AND BRING TO THE BOIL. REDUCE THE HEAT AND COOK FOR 1½ HOURS OR UNTIL TENDER. DRAIN INTO A COLANDER AND TOSS IN A SPLASH OF GOOD OLIVE OIL.

canola or sunflower oil for shallow-frying

1 head cauliflower, cut into florets

2 brown onions, finely sliced

1 piece Lebanese flatbread, torn into bite-sized pieces

olive oil, for drizzling

1½ tablespoons ghee

100 g (3½ oz) slivered almonds

200 g (7 oz) cooked (see note) or drained tinned chickpeas

50 g (1¾ oz) sultanas (golden raisins)

1 bunch coriander (cilantro), leaves picked and roughly chopped

1 bunch flat-leaf (Italian) parsley, leaves picked and roughly chopped

1 bunch basil, leaves torn

DRESSING

1 garlic clove, crushed

150 g (5½ oz) tahini

200 g (7 oz) Greek-style yoghurt

juice of 1 lemon

Serves 4–6 as a starter or light meal
WATERMELON WITH HALOUMI, PINE NUTS, SUMAC & MINT

We sell tons of this in summer. The classic version is made with feta but haloumi is our cheese of choice. It's a fantastic barbecue salad. Just be aware that haloumi gets rubbery once it goes cold so you need to serve and eat this salad straight away.

In a mixing bowl, combine the shallots, herbs, witlof and chilli. Add the lemon juice, olive oil and half the sumac, and season well with salt and pepper. Toss well to combine.

Heat an oiled chargrill pan or heavy-based frying pan to very hot over high heat. Grill the haloumi for a minute on each side, season well with salt and pepper.

To assemble, very gently toss the watermelon, haloumi, salad and pine nuts together and place on a serving platter. Sprinkle with the remaining sumac and drizzle with olive oil. Season to taste.

2 shallots, finely sliced

1 bunch coriander (cilantro), leaves picked

½ bunch mint, leaves picked and torn

2 red witlof (chicory/Belgian endive)

1 long red chilli, deseeded and finely diced

juice of 1 lemon

50 ml (1¾ fl oz) extra-virgin olive oil, plus extra for drizzling

2 tablespoons sumac

250 g (9 oz) haloumi, sliced

¼ watermelon, flesh cut into bite-sized triangles

50 g (1¾ oz) pine nuts, toasted

*Serves 4–6 as a starter
or light meal*

RED SALAD

This is basically a red coleslaw. Paul decided to use everything red he could find, including beetroot and radiccio. It even has red quinoa. It was one of those experiments that you do from time to time that just works beautifully. It looks amazing.

Preheat the oven to 150°C (300°F).

Spread the walnuts onto a baking tray and toast in the oven for 12 minutes, until golden.

Place the quinoa in a saucepan with 1 litre (34 fl oz/4 cups) of water and a pinch of salt. Bring to the boil, then turn down the heat and simmer for 15 minutes until the quinoa is soft and the water has been absorbed.

Place the beetroot in a large saucepan of salted water. Bring to the boil, then reduce to a simmer and cook for 1–1½ hours until the beetroot is tender enough for a knife to pierce the flesh without resistance. Drain and set aside to cool. When cool enough to handle, peel the beetroot by gently rubbing off the skin (make sure you wear kitchen gloves to do this). Cut the beetroot into cubes and set aside.

To make the dressing, combine the lemon juice, salt, pepper and baharat in a small bowl. Slowly whisk in the oil and adjust the seasoning to taste.

Combine the quinoa, beetroot, walnuts and remaining salad ingredients in a large bowl with the dressing. Toss to combine, season with salt and pepper, then transfer to a platter to serve.

150 g (5½ oz/1½ cups) walnuts

300 g (10½ oz) red quinoa

400 g beetroot (beets), trimmed and washed

½ red cabbage, shredded

1 radicchio, finely sliced

1 red onion, finely sliced

1 handful baby beetroot (beet) leaves

6 radishes, finely sliced on a mandoline

250 g (9 oz) red cherry tomatoes, halved

DRESSING

100 ml (3½ fl oz) lemon juice

2 teaspoons salt

1 teaspoon freshly ground pepper

1 tablespoon Baharat (page 182)

200 ml (7 fl oz) olive oil

FENNEL, PEAR, KOHLRABI & WATERCRESS SALAD

This salad is based on a traditional celeriac remoulade with kohlrabi, capers and mayonnaise, but we decided to lighten it up a bit. It's more like a coleslaw now and is fantastic to eat with barbecued meat.

To make the dressing, place all of the ingredients in a small bowl and whisk to combine.

Combine the fennel, pears and kohlrabi with the dressing, then add the remaining ingredients, season to taste and toss lightly.

3 large fennel bulbs, finely sliced on a mandoline

2 pears, each cut into 8 wedges

1 kohlrabi, peeled and cut into matchsticks

2 red witlof (chicory/Belgian endive), trimmed and leaves cut in half lengthways

5 radishes, finely sliced on a mandoline

1 bunch basil, leaves picked

1 bunch watercress sprigs

CRÈME FRAÎCHE DRESSING

200 g (7 oz) crème fraîche

1 garlic clove, crushed

1 tablespoon dijon mustard

pinch of sugar

juice and finely-grated zest of 2 lemons

150 ml (5 fl oz) extra-virgin olive oil

Serves 4–6 as a starter or light meal

BEETROOT, LENTIL & RICOTTA SALATA

We have ten or so different beetroot (beet) salads because, even though everyone seems to love a beetroot salad, they still don't want to eat the same one every day. This version is one of our favourites.

Place the beetroot in a large saucepan of cold salted water and simmer over low heat for 1–1½ hours until tender. Drain and set aside to cool. When cool enough to handle, peel the beetroot and cut into 3 cm (1¼ in) cubes. (Make sure you wear kitchen gloves for this.)

Meanwhile, preheat the oven to 150°C (300°F).

To make the dressing, combine all the ingredients in a small bowl and whisk together.

Add the onion to the dressing and set aside for 30 minutes.

Place the lentils in a large saucepan filled with cold water and simmer for 20–25 minutes over low heat until tender. Drain and spread onto a tray to cool.

Spread the walnuts onto a baking tray and toast in the oven for 12 minutes, until golden. Set aside to cool, then roughly crush.

To assemble the salad, mix the beetroot, dill and lentils together in a bowl. Add the dressing and onion, season to taste and combine well. Spread onto a serving dish and scatter the walnuts and ricotta salata over the top.

10 small beetroot (beets), washed

2 red onions, thinly sliced

400 g (14 oz) puy lentils

100 g (3½ oz/1 cup) walnuts

1 bunch dill, picked

150 g (5½ oz) ricotta salata (salted ricotta), crumbled

CABERNET-WINE DRESSING

100 ml (3½ fl oz) cabernet-wine vinegar

300 ml (10 fl oz) olive oil

2 tablespoons honey

2 teaspoons salt

1 teaspoon pepper

Serves 4–6 as a starter or light meal

VERMICELLI NOODLE SALAD WITH THAI CHILLI DRESSING

Obviously Vietnamese inspired, this is one of the few Asian salads on our list. We love noodle salads, and Asian flavours are as much a part of how we eat in Australia now as European and Middle Eastern ones.

Bring a large saucepan of water to the boil. Remove from the heat, add the rice noodles and let them soak for about 5 minutes. Drain and set aside to cool

To make the dressing, combine all of the ingredients in a small food processer and blend until smooth and well combined.

To make the salad, combine all of the ingredients in a bowl. Add the dressing and toss to combine well. Transfer to a salad bowl and serve.

200 g (7 oz) rice vermicelli noodles

250 g (9 oz) wombok (Chinese cabbage), shredded

4 carrots, cut into matchsticks

100 g (3½ oz) bean spouts

2 bunches coriander (cilantro), leaves picked

1 bunch Thai basil, leaves picked

2 bunches Vietnamese mint, leaves torn

1 bunch mint, leaves torn

½ long white radish (daikon), cut into matchsticks

125 g (4½ oz/½ cup) fried shallots

80 g (2¾ oz/½ cup) peanuts, lightly toasted and roughly chopped

THAI CHILLI DRESSING

1 long red chilli, roughly chopped

juice of 4 limes

50 g (1¾ oz) palm sugar, grated

1 garlic clove, roughly chopped

1 teaspoon fish sauce

125 ml (4 fl oz/½ cup) olive oil

1 handful coriander (cilantro) leaves

GRILLED ZUCCHINI WITH COUSCOUS, SMOKED EGGPLANT & PANGRITATA

Serves 4–6 as a starter or light meal

Pearl (Israeli) couscous (or moghrabieh, as the Lebanese call it), is a fat, round couscous. It has a pasta-like texture and is beautiful to eat.

Preheat the oven to 180°C (350°F). Lightly grease a baking tray.

To make the smoked eggplant, prick the eggplants all over with a fork then cook them directly on the flames of a gas stovetop, turning regularly until very charred all over. Place the eggplants and the garlic cloves on the prepared tray and bake for 30 minutes or until the eggplants have completely collapsed. Set aside to cool. Slice the eggplants open and scoop the flesh into a food processor. Squeeze the roasted garlic out of their skins and add to the eggplant. Start the food processor on low and slowly add the tahini, lemon juice and olive oil. Blend until incorporated and season to taste.

To make the pangritata, toss the bread in a bowl with the lemon zest, garlic, salt and olive oil. Spread onto a greased baking tray and toast in the oven for about 15 minutes until golden brown. Set aside to cool, then crumble into small pieces.

Meanwhile, bring a saucepan of salted water to the boil. Add the couscous and cook for 12 minutes or until al dente. Drain, toss with a little olive oil and spread out onto a baking tray to cool.

Place the eggplant in a colander and toss with a good amount of salt. Allow to sit for 30 minutes to draw out excess moisture and bitterness. Rinse under cold water and pat dry with a clean cloth.

Fill a frying pan about 2 cm (¾ in) full with the canola or sunflower oil and heat until it just starts to smoke. Add the eggplant and fry until golden brown. Remove and drain on paper towel. Repeat with the zucchini.

To assemble, place all the ingredients except the eggplant purée in a salad bowl and toss to combine. Divide the eggplant purée among individual serving plates and top with the salad. Season well and drizzle with a little olive oil and lemon juice.

250 g (9 oz) pearl (Israeli) couscous

olive oil, for drizzling

2 eggplants (aubergines), cut into bite-sized pieces

canola or sunflower oil for shallow-frying

6 zucchini (courgettes), cut into bite-sized pieces

1 bunch flat-leaf (Italian) parsley, leaves picked

1 bunch coriander (cilantro), leaves picked

lemon juice, for drizzling

SMOKED EGGPLANT PURÉE

4 eggplants (aubergines)

6 garlic cloves, skins left on

100 g (3½ oz) tahini

juice of 4 lemons (zest used below)

50 ml (1¾ fl oz) olive oil

PANGRITATA

2 pieces Lebanese flatbread, roughly torn

finely-grated zest of 4 lemons

5 garlic cloves, roughly chopped

1 tablespoon salt

100 ml (7 fl oz) olive oil

Serves 4–6 as a starter or light meal

RISONI SALAD WITH ASPARAGUS, ZUCCHINI, LEMON & RICOTTA

This salad is fresh and delicious and, like grain salads, it's best served at room temperature – so don't go from fridge to table. It needs time to warm to room temperature so you can actually taste everything.

To make the dressing, place all of the ingredients in a bowl and whisk to combine.

Prepare an ice bath by filling a large bowl with water and adding ice cubes.

Bring a large saucepan of salted water to the boil and blanch the asparagus for 1 minute. Remove the asparagus and refresh in the ice bath. Add the risoni to the same saucepan and cook for 15–20 minutes until al dente. Drain and rinse under cold water. Set aside to cool.

When the risoni is completely cool, place in a salad bowl and mix in the dressing and remaining ingredients.

200 g (7 oz) asparagus, trimmed and finely sliced on an angle

500 g (1 lb 2 oz) risoni

4 zucchini (courgettes), cut into matchsticks

250 g (9 oz) fresh or thawed frozen peas

150 g (5½ oz) pine nuts, toasted

1 bunch basil, leaves torn

½ bunch mint, leaves torn

½ bunch dill, roughly chopped

100 g (3½ oz) semi-dried tomatoes, chopped

DRESSING

100 g (3½ oz) fresh ricotta

150 g (5½ oz) Greek-style yoghurt

juice of 3 lemons

zest of 2 lemons

150 ml (5 fl oz) extra-virgin olive oil

Serves 4–6 as a starter or light meal

AVOCADO, CHERRY TOMATO & DUKKAH SALAD

This was another salad that Paul discovered while he was in California. The original had pine nuts in it but we wanted to give this a bit of a Middle Eastern twist, so swapped them for dukkah. You can also use toasted almonds or walnuts.

To make the dressing, combine the honey, mustard, garlic and lime juice in a small bowl. Slowly whisk in the olive oil and season to taste.

Combine the avocado, cherry tomatoes, spinach, coriander and dressing in a bowl and toss gently, being careful not to break up the avocado. Spread onto a serving platter and sprinkle the dukkah over the top. Serve with lime cheeks alongside.

4 avocados, flesh chopped

250 g (9 oz) red cherry tomatoes, halved

250 g (9 oz) yellow cherry tomatoes, halved

2 handfuls baby spinach leaves

3 tablespoons finely-chopped coriander (cilantro) leaves

2 tablespoons Dukkah (page 182)

lime cheeks, to serve

LIME DRESSING

2 tablespoons honey

1 teaspoon dijon mustard

1 garlic clove, crushed

100 ml (3½ fl oz) lime juice

100 ml (3½ fl oz) olive oil

Serves 4–6 as a starter or light meal
FARRO, PERSIAN FETA & ALMOND SALAD

One of our star salads, we first started making this at our restaurant Gorski & Jones. It has great textures and is one of those salads that's even better the next day. We've made this a few times for family functions and every time someone will turn around and say, 'Wow, that's amazing, what's in it?' And that doesn't happen very often. They're quite picky, my family, so if they like it, we're doing something right.

Place the a farro in a large saucepan, cover with 1.5 litres (51 fl oz/6 cups) of water, add the salt and bring to the boil. Reduce the heat and simmer for 15 minutes or until al dente. Drain and rinse under cold water.

Place the ghee in a shallow frying pan over low heat. When melted, add the almonds and cook until golden. This happens quite quickly so make sure you keep your eye on the ball while tossing the almonds around. Drain on paper towel.

In a small bowl, combine the olive oil and the pesto.

To assemble the salad, fold the farro, feta, herbs and almonds together with the pesto in a large serving bowl. Season to taste and serve.

500 g (1 lb 2 oz) pearled farro

1 tablespoon salt

1½ tablespoons ghee

100 g (3½ oz) slivered almonds

1 tablespoon olive oil

4 tablespoons Pesto (page 183)

60 g (2 oz) Persian feta, crumbled

1 small handful dill, roughly chopped

1 small handful basil leaves

1 small handful flat-leaf (Italian) parsley leaves

Serves 4–6 as a starter or light meal
ROASTED PUMPKIN, ROCKET, BALSAMIC ONION & PARMESAN

There's something almost dessert-like when you combine roast pumpkin and caramelised onion. Throw in salty parmesan and peppery rocket (arugula) and you have a superb salad.

Preheat the oven to 180°C (350°F). Line a baking tray with baking paper.

Spread the pumkin onto the prepared tray and drizzle with a little olive oil and season with salt and pepper. Bake for 25 minutes or until tender and golden brown.

Meanwhile, heat the olive oil in a heavy-based oven-proof frying pan over high heat. Add the onions and cook for 2 minutes. Add the vinegar and thyme, reduce the heat to low, season with salt and pepper, and cook for 10 minutes. Transfer the pan to the oven and bake for 15–20 minutes until tender.

To serve, arrange the pumpkin wedges on a platter. Top with the roasted onions and sprinkle the rocket, pine nuts and parmesan over the top.

1 large (about 1.2 kg/2 lb 10 oz) butternut pumpkin (squash), cut into thin wedges

100 ml (3½ fl oz) olive oil, plus extra for drizzling

2 red onions, quartered

250 ml (8½ fl oz/1 cup) balsamic vinegar

4 sprigs thyme, leaves picked

2 handfuls rocket (arugula)

150 g (5½ oz/1 cup) pine nuts, lightly toasted

100 g (3½ oz) shaved Parmigiano Reggiano (or other good parmesan)

SITTING IN

PORK & VEAL MEATBALLS

CHICKPEA, FREGOLA
& FENNEL SOUP

CHICKEN SCHNITZEL

BOLOGNESE

PANCETTA & PEA RISOTTO

SAFFRON & LEEK RISOTTO

PAN-FRIED SALMON WITH TAHINI
DRESSING & WALNUT TARATOR

HOUMOUS

BABA GHANOOJ

KIBBEH

FELAFEL

LADIES' FINGERS

LEBANESE EGGPLANT
CAPONATA

EGGPLANT STUFFED WITH
WALNUTS & GARLIC

YOGHURT & MINT
DUMPLING SOUP

CHICKPEA CORIANDER
FRITTERS

'LITTLE TOMMY'
KOUSSA

MONKS' SOUP

Serves 6–8
PORK & VEAL
MEATBALLS

*The humble meatball has been a part of Alimentari from the time we
had a stove. We've piled them on polenta and squashed them in wraps.
However you have them, they're a hit.*

Preheat the oven to 180°C (350°F).

Heat the extra-virgin olive oil in a wide, heavy-based oven-proof frying pan over medium heat.
Sauté the onion and garlic and cook for about 5 minutes, until softened. Add the tomatoes, salt
and pepper, bring to the boil, cover and simmer for 30 minutes.

Meanwhile, to make the meatballs, combine all of the ingredients in a large mixing bowl. Mix well
with your hands. Roll the mixture into golf ball-sized balls.

Heat the olive oil in a wide, heavy-based pan over medium heat. Fry the meatballs, in batches,
until browned all over, then transfer to the sauce. Place the frying pan in the oven for about
30 minutes.

Serve in a wrap (page 40) or on corn polenta topped with parmesan and fresh basil leaves.

125 ml (4 fl oz/½ cup) extra-virgin olive oil

1 onion, chopped

3 garlic cloves, crushed

2 x 400 g (14 oz) tins diced tomatoes

2 teaspoons salt

1 teaspoon freshly ground black pepper

olive oil for shallow-frying

Corn polenta (page 193), to serve (optional)

shaved parmesan, to serve (optional)

basil leaves, to serve (optional)

MEATBALLS

500 g (1 lb 2 oz) minced (ground) pork

500 g (1 lb 2 oz) minced (ground) veal

1 red chilli, deseeded and chopped

2 sprigs rosemary, leaves finely chopped

1 x 400 g (14 oz) tin diced tomatoes, drained

1 teaspoon sumac

1 teaspoon finely-grated orange zest

1 tablespoon Worcestershire sauce

1 handful basil leaves, chopped

1 handful flat-leaf (Italian) parsley leaves, chopped

1 egg

100 g (3½ oz/1 cup) dry breadcrumbs

Serves 4–6
CHICKPEA, FREGOLA & FENNEL SOUP

This is based on a traditional Sardinian recipe. You can use chicken, fish, vegetable stock or water, though chicken stock is what we prefer.

Heat the oil in a heavy-based saucepan over medium–low heat. Add the onion, diced fennel, carrot, celery, garlic and bay leaves. Sweat, stirring often, for about 5 minutes until the vegetables are translucent (but don't allow them to colour). Add the chickpeas, fregola, grated tomato and the stock or water. Simmer for 30 minutes or until the fregola is al dente.

Season with salt and pepper and stir in the spinach leaves and the fennel fronds (reserve a few for garnishing).

Serve the soup in bowls, garnished with fennel fronds and a drizzle of extra-virgin olive oil.

~~~~~~~~~

NOTE: TO COOK CHICKPEAS, START THE NIGHT BEFORE BY SOAKING 300 G (10½ OZ) DRIED CHICKPEAS IN COLD WATER. THE NEXT DAY, DRAIN THEN RINSE THE CHICKPEAS AND PLACE IN A LARGE SAUCEPAN. COVER WITH FRESH WATER AND BRING TO THE BOIL. REDUCE THE HEAT AND COOK FOR 1½ HOURS OR UNTIL TENDER. DRAIN INTO A COLANDER AND TOSS IN A SPLASH OF GOOD OLIVE OIL.

~~~~~~~~~

NOTE: FREGOLA IS A SARDINIAN PASTA MADE FROM SEMOLINA, AVAILABLE FROM MEDITERRANEAN GROCERS. YOU CAN SUBSTITUTE PEARL (ISRAELI) COUSCOUS OR RISONI IF UNAVAILABLE.

125 ml (4 fl oz/½ cup) olive oil

1 onion, finely diced

2 fennel bulbs, bulbs finely diced and fronds trimmed and chopped

1 carrot, finely diced

3 celery stalks, finely diced

3 garlic cloves, finely chopped

2 bay leaves

500 g (1 lb 2 oz) cooked (see note) or drained tinned chickpeas

300 g (10½ oz) fregola (see note)

5 tomatoes, sliced in half and grated

1.5 litres (51 fl oz/6 cups) water or chicken stock (page 196)

2 cups baby spinach leaves

extra-virgin olive oil, for drizzling

We use these in our Chicken schnitzel wraps (page 43), but they make a great meal with a side salad. Pan-frying definitely gets you the best result here; it makes the schnitzel crunchier and not so oily. If you do want to deep-fry them, make sure the oil is clean and hot so that the cooking time is very quick.

Place the chicken breasts between two sheets of plastic wrap and bash with a meat tenderiser until flattened to about 2 mm (⅛ in) thick. You can leave them whole or cut into smaller pieces.

In a bowl, combine the eggs, milk, garlic and salt and pepper. Place the flour in a second bowl, and in a third bowl, combine the breadcrumbs, lemon zest, parsley and cheese.

Dredge the chicken through the flour and then the egg and breadcrumb mixtures, shaking off any excess between coatings. Set aside on a plate until all of the chicken is coated.

Heat the oil in a large frying pan over medium heat and cook the chicken, in batches, for 2–3 minutes on each side or until golden brown all over. Drain on paper towel.

Serve in a wrap or with a side salad.

4 skinless boneless chicken breasts

4 eggs

1 tablespoon milk

2 garlic cloves, crushed

1 teaspoon salt

1 teaspoon freshly ground black pepper

250 g (9 oz/1⅔ cup) plain (all-purpose) flour

250 g (9 oz/2½ cups) dry breadcrumbs

finely grated zest of 1 lemon

1 large handful flat-leaf (Italian) parsley leaves, finely chopped

100 g (3½ oz) parmesan cheese, grated

canola or sunflower oil for shallow-frying

Serves 6
BOLOGNESE

There are countless recipes around for a good bolognese sauce; this particular one is simple and delicious. There have been a few chefs along the way that have tried to tweak or 'improve' our bolognese, but you can't get much past Alimentari customers. This makes for a hearty, comforting lunch and is a staple on our take-home meals menu.

Place the mushrooms in a small bowl and cover with lukewarm water. Leave to soak for 30 minutes.

Heat the oil in a wide, heavy-based frying pan over medium heat. Sauté the onion, carrot, celery and garlic for about 5 minutes until soft and the onions are translucent. Add the pancetta or prosciutto and cook for another 2 minutes. Drain the mushrooms, discarding the water, then add to the frying pan and cook for 2 minutes.

Add the beef mince and cook, stirring and breaking up clumps with a wooden spoon, for 5–7 minutes or until the liquid has evaporated and the meat is browned.

Stir in the wine and simmer for about 3 minutes, until the liquid has reduced by about three-quarters. Add the tomatoes, crushing them with your hands as you add them to the pan. Bring to the boil then reduce the heat to low. Cover and simmer for 1½ hours.

Season to taste. If desired, serve over gnocchi or fresh pasta.

25 g (1 oz) dried porcini mushrooms

50 ml (1¾ fl oz) olive oil

100 g (3½ oz) onion, finely diced

100 g (3½ oz) carrots, finely diced

100 g (3½ oz) celery, finely diced

2–3 garlic cloves, crushed

150 g (5½ oz) pancetta or prosciutto (or a mix of both), diced

500 g (1 lb 2 oz) minced (ground) beef

200 ml (7 fl oz) red wine

1 x 400 g (14 oz) tin whole tomatoes

1 quantity Potato gnocchi or Fresh pasta (page 190), to serve (optional)

Serves 4
PANCETTA & PEA RISOTTO

We're extremely proud of our risotto. We've managed to package it up as a take-home meal without compromising the quality. We make the packaged product a few minutes off being finished, so our customers are able to follow simple instructions to finish off the process and enjoy a homemade meal.

Bring the stock to a soft boil in a saucepan over medium–high heat.

Meanwhile, heat the oil in a wide, heavy-based frying pan over medium heat. Sauté the onion for about 5 minutes until soft and translucent. Add the pancetta and garlic and cook for about 3–4 minutes, until the pancetta begins to caramelise.

Add the rice and cook, stirring, for about 2 minutes until the rice is toasted and well coated with the oil. Add the wine, scraping any tasty sticky bits up from the bottom of the frying pan. Once most of the wine is absorbed, reduce the heat to low and add a ladleful of stock to the rice and simmer, stirring, until absorbed. Add another ladle, and repeat, simmering and stirring until all of the stock has been added and the rice is al dente. This should take about 20 minutes.

Stir in the peas. Remove from the heat and mix in the butter and parmesan, and season to taste. Serve sprinkled with a little extra parmesan.

2 litres (68 fl oz/8 cups) Chicken stock (page 196)

125 ml (4 fl oz/½ cup) olive oil

1 onion, finely diced

100 g (3½ oz) pancetta, cut into lardons

4 garlic cloves, crushed

370 g (13 oz/2 cups) arborio rice

150 ml (5 fl oz) white wine

150 g (5½ oz) fresh or thawed frozen peas

30 g (1 oz) unsalted butter

75 g (2¾ oz) parmesan cheese, grated, plus extra to serve.

> Serves 4
> # SAFFRON & LEEK RISOTTO

This is a very popular dish with our vegetarian customers. It's packed full of flavour and is delicious as a main or as a side dish. The saffron gives it a lovely colour and an aromatic flavour. It's another one of our Mediterranean Lebanese–Italian fusion dishes.

Bring the stock and saffron to a soft boil in a saucepan over medium–high heat.

Meanwhile, heat the oil in a wide, heavy-based frying pan over medium heat. Sauté the leek and garlic for 3–4 minutes.

Add the rice and cook, stirring, for about 2 minutes until the rice is toasted and well coated with the oil. Add the wine, scraping any tasty sticky bits up from the bottom of the frying pan. Once most of the wine is absorbed, reduce the heat to low and add a ladleful of stock to the rice and simmer, stirring, until absorbed. Add another ladle, and repeat, simmering and stirring until all of the stock has been added and the rice is al dente. This should take about 20 minutes.

Remove from the heat, mix in the butter and parmesan and season to taste.

Pat the leeks dry with paper towel and drizzle with the sunflower oil. Heat a chargrill pan or heavy-based frying pan to hot over high heat. Cook the leeks for about 1 minute, then turn and cook for another minute, until lightly charred. Season well with salt and pepper.

Serve the risotto topped with the charred leeks and sprinkled with extra parmesan.

2 litres (68 fl oz/8 cups) vegetable stock

small pinch of saffron

125 ml (4 fl oz/½ cup) olive oil

3 leeks (about 400 g/14 oz) cleaned and sliced into 1 cm (½ in) discs

4 garlic cloves, crushed

370 g (13 oz/2 cups) arborio rice

150 ml (5 fl oz) white wine

30 g (1 oz) unsalted butter

75 g (2¾ oz) parmesan cheese, grated, plus extra to serve

1 bunch baby leeks, trimmed and washed thoroughly

1 tablespoon sunflower oil

Serves 4

PAN-FRIED SALMON WITH TAHINI DRESSING & WALNUT TARATOR

Tarator is a Middle Eastern walnut and spiced herb mix that's traditionally served with fish. The traditional version of this dish is pretty heavy, as the fish is stuffed with walnuts and then slathered in tahini, which is dense and very rich. This is our lighter take on the classic.

Preheat the oven to 160°C (320°F).

To make the tahini dressing, pound the garlic and salt to a paste using a mortar and pestle. Transfer to a food processor along with the remaining ingredients and process until combined.

Season the salmon with salt and pepper. Heat the olive oil in a large heavy-based ovenproof frying pan over medium–high heat. Add the fish, skin side down, and cook for 3 minutes.

Transfer the pan to the oven for 4 minutes.

Return to the stove over high heat and turn the fish over. Add the butter and cook until the butter is melted and nut brown. Spoon the melted butter over the fish and then remove the fish to drain on paper towel.

To make the tarator, combine the walnuts, chilli and herbs in a small bowl. Dress with a squeeze of lemon and a drizzle of extra-virgin olive oil and toss gently to combine.

Spoon the tahini dressing onto four plates and top with a piece of fish. Garnish with the tarator.

4 x 200 g (7 oz) skin-on salmon fillets

2 tablespoons olive oil

30 g (1 oz) butter

TAHINI DRESSING

1 garlic clove, crushed

1 teaspoon salt

100 g (3½ oz) Greek-style yoghurt

110 g (4 oz/1 cup) tahini

125 ml (4 fl oz/½ cup) lemon juice

125 ml (4 fl oz/½ cup) olive oil

WALNUT TARATOR

100 g (3½ oz/1 cup) walnuts, toasted and chopped

1 red or green chilli, finely chopped

1 handful coriander (cilantro) leaves

1 handful (Italian) parsley leaves

1 small handful mint leaves, roughly torn

½ lemon

extra-virgin olive oil, for drizzling

Serves 8–10
HOUMOUS

This is another classic Lebanese favourite that my mum makes and is always in the fridge. Mum has made all of the Alimentari dips including Labne (page 181) and Baba ghanooj (opposite) from day one. We love spreading lashings of this houmous on our felafel wraps (even though tahini is the more traditional option).

2 garlic cloves, chopped

1½ teaspoons salt

400 g (14 oz) cooked or tinned chickpeas (see notes)

180 g (6½ oz) tahini

150 ml (5 fl oz) lemon juice, plus more if required

extra-virgin olive oil, for drizzling

paprika, chopped flat-leaf (Italian) parsley and diced pickled turnip, to garnish (optional)

Pound the garlic and salt to a paste using a mortar and pestle. Transfer to a food processor, add the chickpeas and process until smooth. With the motor running, slowly add the tahini and lemon juice and keep blending until well combined and smooth. If you want a smoother, thinner dip, slowly add more lemon juice until you achieve the consistency you like.

Spoon the mixture into a bowl, form a well in the middle and drizzle with olive oil. Garnish with the paprika, parsley and turnip, if you wish. Alternatively, this houmous will keep in an airtight container in the fridge for up to 1 week.

NOTE: TO COOK CHICKPEAS, START THE NIGHT BEFORE BY SOAKING 250 G (9 OZ) DRIED CHICKPEAS IN COLD WATER MIXED WITH 1 TEASPOON BICARBONATE OF SODA (BAKING SODA). THE NEXT DAY, DRAIN THEN RINSE THE CHICKPEAS AND PLACE IN A SAUCEPAN. COVER WITH COLD FRESH WATER AND BRING TO THE BOIL. REDUCE THE HEAT TO MEDIUM AND COOK FOR 30 MINUTES OR UNTIL TENDER, REMOVING ANY WHITE FROTH THAT RISES TO THE SURFACE. DRAIN AND SET ASIDE TO COOL.

NOTE: IF USING TINNED CHICKPEAS, FIRST EMPTY THE ENTIRE CONTENTS OF THE TIN, INCLUDING THE WATER, INTO A SAUCEPAN AND BRING TO A GENTLE BOIL OVER MEDIUM HEAT. TRANSFER TO A FOOD PROCESSOR AND PROCEED WITH THE RECIPE.

Serves 8-10
BABA GHANOOJ

If your baba's not smoky, it's not baba! Charring the eggplants (aubergines) is a simple process and well worth doing in order to achieve the amazing smoky flavour of this dip. You can use a stovetop, but to do this properly (like my mum), you really should burn the eggplants on a wood-burning barbecue in your backyard.

Place the eggplants directly over the flame on a gas stove or wood-burning barbecue, turning regularly until completely black and charred all over. Set aside for a few minutes to cool. With gloves on, run the eggplant under cold running water. Holding the stalk, peel away the charred skin and discard. Place the flesh in a colander and set aside for up to 1 hour to completely drain any excess liquid.

Place the eggplant in a blender or food processor. Add the tahini, garlic, lemon juice and salt and blend well until smooth and creamy.

Spoon the mixture into a bowl, form a well in the middle and drizzle with olive oil. Garnish with the tomato and parsley, if you wish. Alternatively, this baba ghanooj will keep in an airtight container in the fridge for up to 1 week.

1 kg (2 lb 3 oz) firm dark eggplants (aubergines)

150 g (5½ oz) tahini

1 garlic clove, crushed

150 ml (5 fl oz) lemon juice

1½ teaspoons salt

extra-virgin olive oil, for drizzling

diced tomato and chopped flat-leaf (Italian) parsley, to garnish (optional)

Clockwise from top left: Houmous (page 108), Felafel (page 113),
Kibbeh (page 112), Ladies' fingers (page 114), Baba ghanooj (page 109),
Pickled turnips (page 195). Centre: Labne (page 181).

Makes about 16
KIBBEH

This is without a doubt my favourite Lebanese dish. There are endless photos of me as a child with kibbeh in my hand. Made in large amounts, kibbeh can be kept frozen and cooked as the perfect last-minute snack for kids or when friends and family drop by. Best of all, no thawing is necessary – just deep- or shallow-fry from frozen. Easy!

220 g (8 oz) fine burghul

200 g (7 oz) lean lamb fillets

2 teaspoons salt

1 teaspoon Baharat (page 182)

canola or sunflower oil for deep-frying

HASHWEE (KIBBEH FILLING)

500 g (1 lb 2 oz) minced (ground) lean lamb

1 large onion, finely diced

1½ teaspoons salt

1 teaspoon Baharat (page 182)

2 tablespoons ghee

25 g (1 oz) pine nuts

To make the hashwee, brown the lamb in a saucepan over medium heat for about 5 minutes, breaking up any clumps with a wooden spoon as you go. Add the onion while there are still juices in the pan and cook until the juices have evaporated. Add the salt and baharat and cook until fragrant. Turn the heat down to low. In a separate saucepan, melt the ghee over medium heat. Add the pine nuts and stir continuously for 3–4 minutes, until golden brown. Add the pine nuts and ghee to the mince, turn the heat up to medium, and cook, stirring, for 1 minute. Remove from the heat and set aside to cool.

Rinse the burghul under cold water. Drain well and set aside for at least 30 minutes.

Place the lamb fillets in a blender or food processor and mince until you have a smooth paste. Transfer to a large mixing bowl. Set yourself up with a bowl of iced water next to the mixing bowl to keep your hands moist whilst kneading the mixture. Add the burghul, salt and baharat to the minced lamb and knead until combined.

To form the kibbeh, first dip your hands in the iced water (to prevent the mixture from sticking) and roll a golf ball-sized ball of the kibbeh mixture using the palms of your hands. Dip your index finger into the water and poke into the ball, creating a hollow. Turn the ball by pressing it against the palm of your hand to create an oval-shaped cup. Place 1 teaspoon of the hashwee into the cup, then bring together the opening and seal. It's easier to dampen your hands at this point and begin to mould the ball in the palm of your hand until it resembles an oval football-shape.

Heat the oil in a deep-fryer, or in a medium-sized saucepan over high heat, until it reaches 175°C (345°F) or until a cube of bread dropped into the oil turns brown in 20 seconds. Fry the kibbeh in batches for 5 minutes or until golden. Drain on paper towel.

We serve these in a wrap, but you can serve as part of a mezze platter or with salad and yoghurt.

Makes 10-12
FELAFEL

It surprises me when I walk into wonderful delis and cafés and see trays of cooked felafel sitting in the cabinets. Felafel is a delight that definitely needs to be cooked and then eaten immediately to really get the best out of those golden, crunchy, slightly spicy, nutty little nuggets. My mum's felafel have graced our menu from day one and, I'm proud to say, served as they should be: cooked fresh to order.

Place the chickpeas and broad beans in a bowl, cover with cold water and soak overnight. Drain and rinse well.

Place about 2 cups of the chickpea and broad bean mix in a food processor along with the onion, garlic, coriander, salt and spices and blend until combined and smooth. Transfer to a large bowl. Blend the remaining chickpeas and broad beans until combined but still a bit chunky. Add to the bowl with the already-blended ingredients and mix in by hand.

Roll the felafel mixture into golf ball-sized balls using the palms of your hands. Gently flatten the balls slightly to form rounds about 2 cm (¾ in) thick.

Heat the oil in a deep-fryer, or in a medium-sized saucepan over high heat, until it reaches 175°C (345°F) or until a cube of bread dropped into the oil turns brown in 20 seconds. Fry the felafel in batches for 3–4 minutes, until crisp and golden. Drain on paper towel.

We serve these in a wrap, but you can serve as part of a mezze platter or with a side of Houmous (page 108) and a garden salad.

200 g (7 oz) dried chickpeas, washed and drained

200 g (7 oz) dried split broad (fava) beans, washed and drained

1 large onion, quartered

4 garlic cloves, roughly chopped

1 bunch coriander (cilantro), including stalks, roughly chopped

2 teaspoons salt

1 teaspoon red chilli powder

1 teaspoon Baharat (page 182)

1 teaspoon ground cumin

canola or sunflower oil for deep-frying

LADIES' FINGERS

Ladies' fingers are a famous Lebanese pastry. This is a savoury version that has always been very popular on our mezze menu. It's important to cook and eat these straight away (no problem really) as they can go a little soggy.

1 x 375 g (13 oz) packet filo pastry

1 quantity Hashwee (see page 112)

canola or sunflower oil for deep-frying

Labne (page 181), to serve

Remove the filo pastry from the packet and cut the roll into thirds. Unroll all three bundles and cut each length in half. Cover the pastry with a damp tea towel to stop it from drying out.

On a clean surface, place three layers of pastry in a vertical strip and two layers in a horizontal strip, to form a crucifix shape. Spoon 1 teaspoon of the hashwee onto the intersection of the pastry strips.

Fold the horizontal ends in to enclose the sides, then, starting at the shortest end near the filling, bring the vertical strip over the hashwee and roll away from you to form an enclosed cigar.

Repeat with the remaining pastry and hashwee.

Heat the oil in a deep-fryer, or in a medium-sized saucepan over high heat, until it reaches 175°C (345°F) or until a cube of bread dropped into the oil turns brown in 20 seconds. Fry the ladies' fingers in batches for about 1 minute or until crisp and golden. Drain on paper towel.

Serve immediately with labne for dipping.

Serves 10–12 as a side
LEBANESE EGGPLANT CAPONATA

This dish is delicious hot or at room temperature and it's lovely both as a side or as a main, eaten with some fresh bread and labne. It sits alongside our antipasto and we serve it with our mezze board at Smith Street.

Place the split chickpeas in a bowl and cover with cold water. Leave to soak overnight, then drain.

Preheat the oven to 200°C (400°F). Heat the grill (broiler) to high.

Place the eggplant on a foil-lined baking tray. Brush both sides lightly with oil and place under the grill. Cook for about 5 minutes on each side until golden brown. Transfer the eggplant to a 35 cm x 25 cm (14 in x 10 in) baking dish.

Heat the olive oil in a saucepan over medium heat and sauté the onion for about 5 minutes, until translucent. Stir in the garlic, chickpeas, tomato and baharat then top with three tomato tins-worth of water. Cover and cook for about 5 minutes.

Slowly pour the mixture over the eggplant (do this gently so the eggplant doesn't float to the surface).Cover with foil and bake for 40 minutes or until the liquid is bubbling.

Remove from the oven and season with salt. You will notice that the eggplant will have broken up into pieces allowing you to easily serve as a side. Serve alongside grilled meat or fish, or as part of a mezze menu. This caponata will keep in the fridge for up to 1 week.

250 g (9 oz) dried split chickpeas

2 large eggplant (aubergines), trimmed, peeled and cut into 3 cm (1¼ in) slices

180 ml (6 fl oz) olive oil, plus extra for brushing

4 large onions, sliced

8 garlic cloves, chopped

2 x 400 g (14 oz) tins diced tomatoes

1½ teaspoons Baharat (page 182)

BEEF BURGER - MILK BUN, GRUYERE, AIOLI, PICKLES
    TOMATO RELISH w CRINKLE CUT CHIPS - 16
BBQ CHICKEN SALAD - HARISSA, FREEKEH, COS MINT, PRESERVED LEMON - 18
SMOKED TROUT SALAD - BEETROOT, WATERCRESS, ALMONDS,
    HORSERADISH CREAM & KIPFLER POTATOES - 17.5
PORK & VEAL MEATBALLS ON SOFT POLENTA OR BRUSCHETTA - 15
SUCKLING PORK LASAGNE w ROQUETTE PESTO - 22
FARRO PASTA - CHERRY TOMATOES w CHILLI, GARLIC & ROQUETTE - 18
PAN FRIED RICOTTA GNOCCHI - MUSHROOM RAGU & PECORINO - 20

Sandwiches & panini available from 10am - sold out
Salads Takeaway Small - 10.5 Large - 15.5

Fresh Wraps available from 12pm until sold out
Soup of the day 9.5

KIBBEH w labne, cucumber, tomato & cos 10.5

FELAFAL w hummus, cucumber, baharat, cos & tomato 10.5

CHICKEN SCHNITZEL w mayo, cos, cucumber, lemon & tomato, cheddar

TRY OUR FAMOUS MEATBALL WRAP w mayo, cheddar, spinach & lemon 10.5

Fills a 1.5 litre (51 fl oz/6 cup) jar
EGGPLANT STUFFED WITH WALNUTS & GARLIC

I've always liked the intricate nature of this dish. There's more to it than just pickling a vegetable and putting it in a jar. Yet it's still simple, looks great on display and is quite impressive as part of a mezze plate.

Prepare an ice bath by filling a large bowl with water and adding ice cubes.

Bring a saucepan of water to the boil over high heat. Add the eggplants and cook for about 5 minutes or until they change to a brown colour. Drain and refresh in the ice bath for 15 minutes. Drain and set aside.

To make the stuffing, combine the walnuts, chilli and garlic in a food processor and blitz until it makes a smooth paste. Transfer to mixing bowl then stir in the salt and oil.

Make an incision along each eggplant ensuring the ends remain intact. Spoon in a teaspoon of the filling and gently press into the cavity.

Place the eggplants into a large sterilised jar with the cut sides facing upwards. In large a bowl, dissolve the salt into 1 litre (34 fl oz/4 cups) of water (see note below). Stir in the vinegar, then pour over the eggplant.

Allow to sit, uncovered, for 48 hours. Top with the oil then cover tightly with the lid.

Store in a cool, dark place for 2 weeks before using. After opening, these stuffed eggplants will keep in an airtight container in the pantry for years.

~~~~~~~~~

NOTE: TO ENSURE THE PICKLING BRINE CONTAINS ENOUGH SALT, PLACE A WHOLE EGG IN THE BOWL WITH THE SALT AND WATER: IF THE EGG FLOATS, THAT MEANS THERE IS ENOUGH SALT. ADD MORE IF THE EGG SINKS.

2.5 kg (5½ lb) small Japanese eggplant (aubergines)

about 1 tablespoon salt

500 ml (17 fl oz/2 cups) white-wine vinegar

60 ml (2 fl oz/¼ cup) olive oil

STUFFING

200 g (7 oz/2 cups) walnuts

5 garlic cloves, chopped

6 long red chillis, roughly chopped

1 tablespoon salt

1 tablespoon olive oil

Serves 6
YOGHURT & MINT DUMPLING SOUP

Yoghurt soup is a Mediterranean classic and everyone has their own take on it. This is a Lebanese version. Some prefer dumplings that are more like gnocchi but I think the lamb filling really makes this dish. Another meal that's lovely both hot or at room temperature.

To make the filling, combine the ingredients in a bowl. Set aside.

For the dumplings, combine the flour and salt in a mixing bowl and gradually add water, mixing until it comes together into a dough. Turn out onto a floured work surface and knead well. Roll out to about 3 mm (⅛ in) thick and then cut out rounds using a 5 cm (2 in) cutter (or a liqueur glass).

Flatten each round slightly and place ½ teaspoon of the filling into the centre. Fold over to seal the edges forming a semi circle. Pinch the edges together to seal.

Place the yoghurt, flour and egg in a large saucepan. Combine using an electric beater or whisk. Place the saucepan over low heat and, stirring constantly, bring to the boil. Add the water and bring to the boil again. Stir in the rice and salt. Carefully add the dumplings and cook, stirring occasionally, for 5 minutes. Add the garlic, ghee and dried mint. Cook for a further 15 minutes or until the rice is cooked.

1 kg (2 lb 3 oz) plain yoghurt

1 tablespoon plain (all-purpose) flour

1 egg

1 litre (34 fl oz/4 cups) boiling water

50 g (1¾ oz/¼ cup) long-grain rice

1 teaspoon salt

2 large garlic cloves, crushed

1 tablespoon ghee

1 teaspoon dried mint

FILLING

1 tablespoon ghee

1 onion, chopped

450 g (1 lb) minced (ground) lean lamb

2 teaspoons salt

½ teaspoon Baharat (page 182)

1 tablespoon finely chopped mint

DUMPLINGS

300 g (10½ oz/2 cups) plain (all-purpose) flour

½ teaspoon salt

Makes 24
CHICKPEA CORIANDER FRITTERS

A traditional Lebanese dish that's normally only served on Good Friday. These fritters are meant to be a food that represents suffering or mourning – but they're great with a cold beer.

Place the split chickpeas in a bowl and cover with cold water. Leave to soak overnight then drain.

Place the burghul in a bowl and cover with cold water. Leave to soak for 2 hours then drain.

Bring a large saucepan of salted water to the boil. Add the potatoes and cook for 20 minutes. Drain then mash.

Combine all of the ingredients except the oil in a large mixing bowl. Gradually add about 750 ml (25½ fl oz/3 cups) of water until the mixture comes together enough to form into patties. Roll into golf ball-sized balls using the palms of your hands. Gently flatten the balls to form patties.

Heat the oil in a deep-fryer, or in a medium-sized saucepan over high heat, until it reaches 175°C (345°F) or until a cube of bread dropped into the oil turns brown in 20 seconds. Fry the fritters in batches for 2–3 minutes on each side until crisp and golden. Drain on paper towel.

440 g (15½ oz/2 cups) dried split chickpeas

475 g (1 lb 1 oz/3 cups) fine burghul

3 potatoes, peeled and chopped

1 large onion, diced

4 spring onions (scallions), sliced

1 small handful flat-leaf (Italian) parsley leaves, roughly chopped

1 small handful coriander (cilantro) leaves, roughly chopped

385 g (13½ oz) plain (all-purpose) flour

2½ teaspoons Baharat (page 182)

2½ teaspoons salt

canola or sunflower oil for deep-frying

Serves 5

'LITTLE TOMMY' KOUSSA

Koussa is typically made with a rice and minced lamb filling, however Dolores and I recognised the need for more vegetarian options for our customers. Hence, our meat-free 'Little Tommy' koussa was born. Eaten hot or at room temperature, this dish can be served simply with a dollop of yoghurt and some fresh Lebanese bread. For best results you will need a specialised utensil called a manakra (see note) to remove the core of the marrow prior to filling them. If you can't find one, you can use an apple corer, but it won't be as easy to use.

To make the stuffing, first place the split chickpeas in a bowl and cover with cold water. Leave to soak overnight then drain. Combine with the remaining ingredients and set aside.

Wash the marrows under running water. Cut off the ends to expose the core. Carefully mark out circles around the exposed cores using a manakra tool, then use the tool to hollow out the marrows.

Half-fill each marrow with the stuffing, pushing it gently into the centre, being careful not to overfill (or the marrow may burst during cooking).

Tip the the tinned tomatoes into the bottom of a large saucepan. Place the marrows on top, sprinkle with the salt and cover with cold water. Mix in the tomato paste and bring to the boil over medium heat. Simmer for 45 minutes until the marrows are tender.

Serve in a bowl with the sauce, a dollop of labne or yoghurt and a side of fresh flatbread.

~~~~~~~~~

NOTE: A MANAKRA RESEMBLES A LONG, THIN APPLE CORER. YOU CAN BUY THEM FROM MIDDLE EASTERN GROCERS.

10 small baby marrows or zucchini (courgettes)

1 x 400 g (14 oz) tin diced tomatoes

1 tablespoon salt

2 tablespoons tomato paste

Labne (page 181) or Greek-style yoghurt, to serve (optional but highly recommended)

fresh Lebanese flatbread, to serve (optional)

STUFFING

220 g (8 oz/1 cup) dried split chickpeas

200 g (7 oz/1 cup) long-grain rice

2 tomatoes, diced

1 onion, diced

3 large handfuls flat-leaf (Italian) parsley leaves, chopped

1 handful mint, chopped

2 teaspoons salt

1 teaspoon Baharat (page 182)

2 tablespoons lemon juice

80 ml (2½ fl oz/⅓ cup) olive oil

Serves 8
MONKS'SOUP

Monks' soup is a Lebanese dish traditionally eaten only on Good Friday. Which is a shame, because the borderline-sour taste is so flavoursome and incredibly moreish. It's Good Friday a lot at my house.

To make the spinach kibbeh filling, heat the oil in a frying pan over medium heat. Add the onion and fry fry until translucent, then add the spinach and cook until softened. Add the baharat and salt, and cook, stirring, until the spinach has wilted.

To make the dumpling dough, first rinse the burghul under cold water and drain well. Combine with the other ingredients and gradually add water until the mixture forms a dough. (This mixture will be used to make one spinach kibbeh per person, and the remainder to make the dumplings.)

Set yourself up with a bowl of iced water. To form the kibbeh, first dip your hands in the water (to prevent the mixture from sticking) and roll a golf ball-sized ball of the dumpling mixture using the palms of your hands.

Dip your index finger into the water and poke into the ball, creating a hollow. Turn the ball by pressing it against the palm of your hand to create an oval-shaped cup. Place 1 teaspoon of the spinach into the cup, then bring together the opening and seal. It's easier to dampen your hands at this point and begin to mould the ball in the palm of your hand until it resembles an oval football-shape. Make one kibbeh per person.

Roll the remaining dumpling mixture into marble-sized balls. Set aside.

Rinse the lentils under cold water and drain well. Place in a large saucepan and cover with 2.5 litres (85 fl oz/10 cups) of water and bring to the boil over medium heat. Once boiling add another 500 ml (17 fl oz/2 cups) of cold water (this prevents the lentils from splitting), then cover and simmer for 15 minutes.

Carefully add the kibbeh and dumplings, then stir in the garlic, pomegranate molasses, salt and oil. Cover and cook over medium heat for a further 30 minutes.

---

90 g (3¼ oz) ½ cup brown lentils

5 garlic cloves, crushed

3 tablespoons pomegranate molasses

3 teaspoons salt

2 tablespoons olive oil

SPINACH KIBBEH FILLING

2 tablespoons olive oil

1 onion, diced

½ bunch spinach, washed and roughly chopped

¼ teaspoon Baharat (page 182)

¼ teaspoon salt

DUMPLINGS

220 g (8 oz/1½ cups) fine burghul

1 large onion, finely chopped

1 tablespoon finely chopped flat-leaf (Italian) parsley

1 tablespoon finely chopped mint

½ teaspoon freshly ground black pepper

1 teaspoon Baharat (page 182)

225 g (8 oz/1½ cups) plain (all-purpose) flour

2 teaspoons salt

LATER

FROM THE
WOODFIRE

EGGPLANT PARMIGIANA

ROASTED POTATOES WITH ROSEMARY & GARLIC

WOOD-FIRED SUCKLING PIG

PORK & FENNEL LASAGNE

RICOTTA-STUFFED EGGPLANT 'CANNELLONI'

SLOW-COOKED LAMB SHOULDER WITH
SKORDALIA & CORIANDER YOGHURT NAAN

SAMBUSIC

WHOLE SNAPPER IN CRAZY WATER

COQ AU VIN

ROAST CHICKEN WITH HARISSA
& PRESERVED LEMON

LEMON & GARLIC CHICKEN WINGS

Serves 6–8

EGGPLANT PARMIGIANA

This is a very popular vegetarian take on lasagne. Using really fresh ingredients makes a huge difference to the quality of this dish. Do use scamorza if you can – it's a little more expensive than fior di latte, but it's well worth it for the delicious smoky flavour.

Preheat the oven to 200°C (400°F). Line two large trays with baking paper.

Spread the eggplant onto the trays, season well and drizzle with olive oil. Bake for 15 minutes, turning once, until lightly browned. Set aside.

Reduce the oven to 175°C (345°F).

Heat the sugo in a medium-sized saucepan over medium heat.

Spread a layer of sugo over the bottom of a 35 cm × 20 cm (14 in x 8 in) baking dish. Top with a layer of eggplant slices, sprinkle with parmesan and then a layer of scamorza or fior di latte. Repeat, scattering the second layer with some basil leaves. You should get three layers. When you get to the top layer, arrange the eggplant, tomato, fior de latte and basil in overlapping rows.

Bake in the oven for 20 minutes or until golden. Allow to cool for a few minutes before serving.

3 large eggplants (aubergines), cut into 1 cm (½ in) thick rounds

olive oil, for drizzling

2 litres (68 fl oz/8 cups) Tomato sugo (page 183)

400 g (14 oz) parmesan cheese, grated

3 balls (about 375 g/13 oz) smoked scamorza or fior di latte (fresh mozzarella), sliced

1 bunch basil, leaves picked

4 tomatoes, sliced

Serves 6–8 as a side
ROASTED POTATOES WITH ROSEMARY & GARLIC

A fancy version of a pretty standard dish. This involves an unusual step of boiling the rosemary and garlic with the potatoes to infuse the flavours before you even start roasting. The ghee takes the potatoes to a level of crispness that you just can't get with normal butter.

Preheat the oven to 200°C (400°F).

Place the potatoes in a large saucepan and just cover with cold water. Add half the salt and the garlic and rosemary.

Cook for 25 minutes or until the potatoes are tender. Drain in a colander and transfer the potatoes, rosemary and garlic to a roasting pan. Add the ghee and remaining salt and season with freshly ground black pepper. Bake for 15 minutes or until the potatoes are crisp and golden brown. Reduce the heat to 180°C (350°F) and cook for a further 15 minutes.

1 kg (2 lb 3 oz) floury potatoes (such as desiree, sebago or coliban), peeled and cut into eighths

100 g (3½ oz) salt

1 head garlic, broken into seperate cloves, skins left on

½ bunch rosemary

250 ml (8½ fl oz/1 cup) melted ghee

Serves 10–12
WOOD-FIRED SUCKLING PIG

We're lucky to have an incredible wood-fired oven at Smith Street, which produces the most amazing roast suckling pig. We know that not everyone has one of these in their backyard, so here's a version for you to cook in a regular oven.

Preheat the oven to 180°C (350°F).

Using a mortar and pestle or small food processor, crush the fennel seeds, salt and rosemary until combined.

To ensure that the flavour gets right into the meat, you should first score the pig skin. Using a very sharp knife, make long diagonal slits across the skin in opposite directions to score diamond shapes. Be careful not to cut down into the flesh.

Rub the pig with oil, inside and out, then cover entirely with the fennel seed mixture.

Place the pig, belly side down with legs extended, onto a large baking tray fitted with a rack. Wrap the ears, tail and snout with baking paper and then foil, to protect them from burning.

Transfer to the oven and cook for about 2½ hours or until the limbs feel loose when you move them. Be sure to check regularly that the pig is browning and crisping nicely.

Increase the heat to 220°C (430°F) and cook for a further 15–20 minutes or until the skin is golden and crisp.

Remove from the oven and set aside to rest for about 15–20 minutes.

Serve with salad or with crusty bread.

100 g (3½ oz) fennel seeds

65 g (2¼ oz/½ cup) sea salt

¼ cup rosemary leaves

1 x 8 kg suckling pig

125 ml (4 fl oz/½ cup) olive oil

salad or crusty bread, to serve (optional)

Serves 8

PORK & FENNEL LASAGNE

This is the leader of the pack, based on a recipe by chef Chris Kerr who Paul worked with at Benito's. This lasagne really put our take-home meals on the map. The fennel seed is a delicious addition – it's fragrant and adds lightness to what is often a heavy meal.

Preheat the oven to 180°C (350°F).

Heat the oil in a large heavy-based saucepan or casserole dish with a well-fitting lid over medium heat. Add the onion, garlic and fennel seeds and sauté for about 5 minutes, until the onion has softened. Add the salt and pepper.

Add the pork mince. Fry for 5–7 minutes, breaking up any clumps with a wooden spoon as you go, until the liquid has evaporated and the meat has browned. Stir in the wine and simmer for about 3 minutes, until the liquid has reduced by about three-quarters. Add the tinned tomatoes and bring to the boil. Reduce the heat to low, cover and simmer for 1½ hours.

If using fresh pasta, roll out the dough and cut into lengths to fit a 35 cm x 30 cm (14 in x 12 in) baking dish.

To assemble the lasagne, spread enough meat sauce to cover the bottom of the dish. Cover with a layer of pasta, then top with one third of the béchamel. Repeat the layers of meat, pasta and béchamel, ending with a béchamel layer at the top (you should get three layers). Top with the cheese and basil leaves.

Bake for 35 minutes or until the top is golden brown. Allow to cool for a few minutes before serving.

125 ml (4 fl oz/½ cup) extra-virgin olive oil

1 onion, diced

4 garlic cloves, crushed

2 tablespoons fennel seeds

1 tablespoon salt

1 tablespoon freshly ground black pepper

1 kg (2 lb 3 oz) minced (ground) pork

200 ml (7 fl oz) dry white wine

2 x 400 g (14 oz) tins diced tomatoes

½ quantity Fresh pasta dough (page 190) or 500 g (1 lb 2 oz) instant lasagne sheets

½ quantity Béchamel sauce (page 184)

100 g (3½ oz) freshly grated parmesan cheese

2 x 125 g (4½ oz) balls fior di latte (fresh mozzarella), sliced

1 large handful basil leaves

RICOTTA-STUFFED EGGPLANT 'CANNELLONI'

When we had our restaurant, Gorski & Jones, we used to make a different antipasto every day. This was one of the dishes we made as part of a daily changing selection.

Preheat the oven to 180°C (350°F).

Place the eggplant in a colander and season liberally with salt. Toss, then leave for 30 minutes to draw out excess moisture and bitterness. Rinse under cold water and pat dry with a clean cloth.

Heat a little oil in a frying pan over medium heat. Fry the eggplant for 2 minutes on each side or until golden. Remove and set aside to drain on paper towel.

In a mixing bowl, combine the ricotta, currants, pine nuts, parsley and lemon juice and zest. Season with salt and pepper.

On a clean work surface, lay out the eggplant slices. Place a tablespoon of the ricotta mixture onto each slice and then roll up like a cigar. Place the rolls into a 35 cm x 25 cm (14 in x 10 in) baking dish, sitting them close together with the seam side down.

Cover the eggplant cigars evenly with the tomato sugo and top with the parmesan and basil leaves. Season well and bake for 30 minutes or until the sugo is bubbling and the cheese has melted.

Remove from the oven and allow to cool for a few minutes before serving.

3 eggplants (aubergines), trimmed and cut lengthways into slices 5 mm (¼ in) thick

vegetable oil, for frying

400 g (14 oz) fresh ricotta

100 g (3½ oz) currants

100 g (3½ oz) pine nuts, toasted and chopped

2 large handfuls flat-leaf (Italian) parsley leaves, chopped

juice and finely-grated zest of 2 lemons

1 bunch basil, leaves torn

500 ml (17 fl oz/2 cups) Tomato sugo (page 185)

100 g (3½ oz) parmesan cheese, grated

Serves 4

SLOW-COOKED LAMB SHOULDER WITH SKORDALIA & CORIANDER YOGHURT NAAN

We cook this at home all the time. Skordalia is better than mashed potato because it has a real kick of garlic, which works beautifully with the lamb.

In a small bowl, combine the ras el hanout, garlic, rosemary, olive oil, salt and pepper. Rub the lamb shoulder all over with the mix. Cover and refrigerate for 3 hours or overnight.

Preheat the oven to 110°C (230°F).

Place the lamb in a roasting pan along with the chicken stock and a few extra garlic cloves. Cover tightly with foil and roast for 6 hours. Uncover and roast for another 30 minutes to allow the skin to crisp up.

Meanwhile, to make the naan, place all of the ingredients except the oil into a bowl and mix until combined. Tip onto a clean work surface and knead for 2 minutes. Cover with plastic wrap and rest for 1 hour. Divide the dough into eight even-sized balls and roll out on a well-floured work surface into rounds 2 mm (⅛ in) thick. Just before serving, heat a little oil in a frying pan over medium heat and fry the naan, one at a time, for 2 minutes on each side or until golden. Set aside and keep warm.

To make the skordalia, place the potatoes in a saucepan with half the salt and enough cold water to cover. Bring to the boil then simmer for 30 minutes or until tender. Drain. Pass the potato through a potato ricer (or mash with a potato masher until very smooth) and transfer to a bowl. Pound the garlic and remaining salt to a smooth paste using a mortar and pestle and stir through the potato. Slowly stir in the oil and lemon juice until smooth and creamy. Season to taste.

To serve, squeeze lemon juice over the lamb, then shred the meat and discard the bones. Spoon a generous dollop of skordalia onto each plate and top with the lamb. Serve the naan alongside and, if desired, a salad such as tabouli.

~~~~~~~~~~

NOTE: RAS EL HANOUT IS A NORTH AFRICAN SPICE MIX. IT IS AVAILABLE FROM GOOD DELIS AND SOME SUPERMARKETS.

50 g (1¾ oz/½ cup) ras el hanout (see note)

8 garlic cloves, crushed, plus extra whole cloves for roasting

2 sprigs rosemary, leaves roughly chopped

200 ml (7 fl oz) olive oil

3 tablespoons salt

3 tablespoons freshly ground black pepper

3 kg (6 lb 10 oz) bone-in lamb shoulder

750 ml (25½ fl oz/3 cups) Chicken stock (page 196)

2 lemon halves, for squeezing

salad, such as tabouli, to serve (optional)

YOGHURT NAAN

600 g (1 lb 5 oz/4 cups) self-raising flour

2 teaspoons salt

2 teaspoons baking powder

300 g (10½ oz/1¼ cups) Greek-style yoghurt

150 ml (5 fl oz) warm water

2 large handfuls coriander (cilantro) leaves, chopped

canola oil, for frying

SKORDALIA

4 medium-sized potatoes

2 teaspoons salt

7 garlic cloves

125 ml (4 fl oz/½ cup) extra-virgin olive oil

2 tablespoons lemon juice

Slow-cooked lamb shoulder with skordalia
& coriander yoghurt naan (page 139)

Makes 10–12 pies
SAMBUSIC

Traditionally, sambusic are small canapé-sized bites. However, super-sizing them proved to be a great idea. Pair with some labne and you have yourself a delicious meal.

Preheat the oven to 260°C (500°F) or the highest temperature it will go. Grease two large baking trays.

Divide the dough in half and work with one piece at a time. Roll out onto a well-floured work surface into a rectangle about 3 mm (⅛ in) thick. Cut out circles using a 12 cm (4¾ in) cutter. Collect the offcuts and roll out again to use up all of the dough. You should get 10–12 circles.

Spoon 2 tablespoons of the hashwee into the centre of each dough circle. Fold the pastry over to form a semi-circle, then press lightly to push out air and seal the edge. Starting at one end, make a series of small folds to crimp the edge (see photos on pages 46–47).

Place the pies onto the prepared baking trays and bake for 20 minutes or until golden.

Allow to cool for a few minutes before serving with a bowl of labne alongside (if desired).

1 quantity Lebanese pie dough (page 188)

1 quantity Hashwee (see page 112)

Labne (page 181), to serve (optional)

Serves 4–6
WHOLE SNAPPER
IN CRAZY WATER

This is another dish we do in the wood-fired oven. It's a quick, simple, tasty recipe and it feeds masses. Crazy water is a classic Italian cooking technique with all the ingredients plus the fish cooked in a broth. I love this dish because you get the golden roastedness of the fish but also the steaming effect from the broth as well. Crazy good.

Preheat the oven to 200°C (400°F).

Heat the oil in a very large frying pan over medium heat. Sweat the onion and chopped fennel for 2 minutes to soften. Add the garlic and chilli and cook for 1 minute before adding the wine and 500 ml (17 fl oz/2 cups) of water. Reduce the heat to low and simmer for 5–10 minutes until the liquid has reduced by half. Season with salt and pepper and set aside to cool.

Place the fish side-by-side in a large baking dish. Add the liquid and top with the cherry tomatoes, shaved fennel, olives and capers. Season lightly and bake for 15–20 minutes until cooked (check by inserting a knife into the thickest part of the fish, the flesh should be white and firm).

To serve, garnish the fish with the fennel fronds and pollen (if using) and drizzle with a good glug of extra-virgin olive oil.

~~~~~~~~

NOTE: FENNEL POLLEN IS MADE FROM DRIED FENNEL FLOWERS. IT IS AVAILABLE FROM GOOD FOOD STORES.

2 tablespoons olive oil

½ onion, finely diced

1 fennel bulb, half finely chopped and half sliced on a mandoline, fronds picked

5 garlic cloves, chopped

½ long red chilli, chopped

500 ml (17 fl oz/2 cups) dry white wine

2 x 500 g (1 lb 2 oz) whole baby snappers, scaled and cleaned (ask your fishmonger to do this)

200 g (7 oz) cherry tomatoes, cut in half

90 g (3 oz/½ cup) kalamata olives (we use wild olives)

1 tablespoon salted capers

pinch of fennel pollen, optional (see note)

extra-virgin olive oil, for drizzling

Serves 6
COQ AU VIN

This might sound complicated and fancy but it's an easy and simply unbeatable Sunday lunch, and delicious on a cold wintery night with your favourite glass of red. Don't be tight with the wine you use for cooking – the darker and richer the better.

Place the chicken in a large bowl and cover with the wine, thyme, bay leaves and half of the garlic. Cover and refrigerate for at least 3 hours or overnight.

Preheat the oven to 160°C (320°F).

Heat the oil in a large casserole dish over high heat. Season the chicken then sear, in batches, until golden brown (reserve the marinade). Set aside on a plate. Reduce the heat to medium and cook the mushrooms, shallots, carrot, celery and kaiserfleisch for 5–6 minutes until lightly coloured. Stir in the remaining garlic and cook for 1 minute.

Deglaze the pan with the reserved marinade and the chicken and beef stocks. Add the chicken and bring to the boil. Cover and place in the oven for 1 hour.

Garnish with thyme and serve on a bed of mashed potato.

1.6 kg (3½ lb) whole free-range chicken, cut into 8 pieces

500 ml (17 fl oz/2 cups) red wine

2 thyme sprigs, plus extra to garnish

2 fresh bay leaves

3 garlic cloves, thinly sliced

125 ml (4 fl oz/½ cup) olive oil

500 g (1 lb 2 oz) button mushrooms

12 shallots

1 large carrot, finely diced

2 celery stalks, finely diced

50 g (1¾ oz) kaiserfleisch or other bacon, cut into thin slices

125 ml (4 fl oz/½ cup) Chicken stock (page 196)

125 ml (4 fl oz/½ cup) beef stock

mashed potato, to serve

Serves 4-6
ROAST CHICKEN WITH HARISSA & PRESERVED LEMON

We sell a huge amount of roast chickens, which we cook on a rotisserie that we had imported from France for the Smith Street store. It's the most ridiculously overpriced piece of equipment we've ever bought, and it will probably never make its money back – but we don't care, because we love it and it makes the most beautiful roast meats and vegetables. The harissa and preserved lemon in this recipe gives a simple family classic a fantastic Middle Eastern spin.

Coat the chicken all over with the harissa, rubbing the paste under the skin. Season the chicken with salt and pepper, inside and out. Wrap tightly with plastic wrap and refrigerate for at least 3 hours or overnight.

Cut one or more of the garlic bulbs in half cross ways and place in the chicken cavity along with the preserved lemon and a sprig of thyme. Tie the legs together with kitchen twine and tuck the wings under. Leave the chicken on the bench for 20 minutes to come to room temperature.

Preheat the oven to 260°C (500°F) or the highest temperature it will go.

Place the chicken on a rack set in a roasting pan and top with the remaining thyme. Place the remaining garlic and the lemon halves in the roasting pan. Cook for 10 minutes to brown the outside of the chicken. Reduce the temperature to 160°C (320°F) and cook for 45 minutes or until juices run clear when a knife is inserted into the thickest part of the thigh.

To serve, place chicken on a board or platter and garnish with lemon, garlic and thyme. If you like (and we highly recommend that you do) accompany with Roasted potatoes with rosemary & garlic.

1.5 kg (3 lb 5 oz) whole free-range chicken

3 tablespoons Harissa paste (page 181)

1 tablespoon salt

1 tablespoon freshly ground black pepper

1 Preserved lemon (page 195)

3 thyme sprigs

2–4 garlic bulbs

2–3 lemons, cut in half

Roasted potatoes with rosemary & garlic (page 133), to serve (optional)

Serves 6 (or 1!)
LEMON & GARLIC CHICKEN WINGS

This was one of my favourite dishes growing up. I don't even like wings but I love these. They're ridiculous. My mum often makes this dish as my daughter loves it. The meat literally falls off the bone and the lemony, garlicky flavour is always guaranteed to make you reach for another.

Preheat the oven to 260°C (500°F) or the highest temperature it will go.

Wash the wings and place in a large bowl. Season with salt and toss with the lemon slices.

Place the wings snugly into a baking tray. Drizzle with the olive oil and place in the oven for about 40 minutes or until browned.

Carefully turn the wings over. Combine the garlic paste and the lemon juice and pour over the wings. Return to the oven and cook for a further 15 minutes.

Transfer the wings to a serving platter and garnish with the coriander and nigella seeds.

Eat straight away. If you're not going to eat the wings immediately, leave them in the tray and cover with foil to prevent drying out.

18 chicken wings cut in half at the joint (you can ask your butcher to do this for you)

1 lemon, finely sliced

1 tablespoon olive oil

150 ml (5 fl oz) Garlic paste (page 180)

200 ml (7 fl oz) lemon juice

1 small handful coriander (cilantro) leaves, finely chopped

1 teaspoon nigella seeds

SWEETS

CHOCOLATE FONDANT MUFFINS

RED VELVET CAKE

BOMBOLONI

CHOCOLATE PEANUT-BUTTER
BROWNIES

FLOURLESS CHOCOLATE
HAZELNUT CAKE

LADIES' ARMS

BAKLAWA

ZUCCHINI & WALNUT CAKE

LEMON TEA CAKES

CRÈME CARAMEL

MANERA'S APPLE CAKE

Makes 12

CHOCOLATE FONDANT MUFFINS

Basically a chocolate self-saucing pudding turned into a muffin, this treat is the gift that keeps on giving. They're best served straight out of the oven. Just add ice cream for a decadent dessert.

Preheat the oven to 150°C (300°F). Line one 12-hole or two 6-hole cupcake tins with paper cases.

Melt the chocolate and butter together in a large heatproof bowl set over a saucepan of simmering water. Stir until smooth and combined. Remove from the heat.

In a separate bowl, whisk the sugar and eggs together. Add to the chocolate mixture and stir until combined. Sift the flour and cocoa powder into the chocolate mixture, stirring well until you have a lovely gooey batter with no lumps.

Half-fill the paper cases with the batter. Bake for 20 minutes or until firm to the touch but still sticky in the centre.

If desired, dust with icing sugar and top with chocolate curls.

300 g (10½ oz) dark cooking chocolate

300 g (10½ oz) butter

300 g (10½ oz) caster (superfine) sugar

8 eggs

90 g (3 oz) plain (all-purpose) flour

90 g (3 oz) cocoa powder

chocolate curls and icing (confectioners') sugar, to decorate (optional)

Serves 8–16

RED VELVET CAKE

This is classic old-school Americana and it looks spectacular. This recipe is for a whole cake but at Alimentari we serve them cup cake-sized, still with the same cream cheese icing.

Preheat the oven to 150°C (300°F). Grease and line the base and side of a 20 cm (8 in) round cake tin with baking paper.

In the bowl of an electric mixer fitted with a paddle attachment, mix the oil, sugar and eggs until well combined.

In a separate bowl, sift the flour, cocoa powder and bicarbonate of soda together. In another bowl, mix the buttermilk, food colouring, vanilla extract and vinegar together.

Add one third of the dry ingredients to the oil and egg mix. Carefully fold in, then add one third of the buttermilk mix. Repeat this two or more times until all the flour and buttermilk mixtures are completely added to produce a smooth, glossy cake batter.

Pour into the lined tin and bake for 1 hour or until a skewer inserted into the middle comes out clean. (Cooking times may vary according to your oven.)

Turn out onto a wire rack to cool. Using a serrated knife, carefully slice across the top crust of the cake. Set aside to be used for crumbs later on.

To make the icing, bring the cream to the boil in a saucepan over medium heat. Remove from the heat and whisk in the white chocolate, stirring until melted and smooth. Set aside to cool. In a separate bowl, beat the cream cheese until smooth. Gradually add the cooled cream mixture to the cream cheese, beating to combine. Add the vanilla and beat until smooth.

Using a serrated knife, carefully slice the cake into three layers.

To assemble the cake, carefully place the bottom layer of cake onto your chosen platter. Spread about one quarter of the icing onto the base, covering it right to the edges. Gently place the second layer on top and repeat. Finish with the top layer and generously cover the entire cake with the remaining icing. Crumble the reserved cake crust to produce fine cake crumbs. Press into the side of the cake and lightly sprinkle over the top.

This cake is best eaten at room temperature.

220 ml (7½ fl oz) canola oil

225 g (8 oz/1 cup) sugar

2 eggs

265 g (9½ oz) plain (all-purpose) flour

2 teaspoons cocoa

1 teaspoon bicarbonate of soda (baking soda)

150 ml (5 fl oz) buttermilk

2 tablespoons red food colouring

1 teaspoon vanilla extract

1 teaspoon vinegar

CREAM CHEESE ICING

100 ml (3½ fl oz) thickened (whipping) cream

150 g (5½ oz) good-quality white chocolate, broken into pieces

500 g (1 lb 2 oz) cream cheese, softened

1 teaspoon vanilla extract

Makes about 14

BOMBOLONI

Everybody loves bomboloni. You can eat them just as they are, or you can fill them with Nutella, custard, fig jam, raspberry jam – it doesn't matter, they'll still walk out the door.

In a small bowl, combine the yeast with the warm water and leave to sit for 10 minutes until frothy.

Place the zest and sugar in the bowl of an electric mixer fitted with a paddle attachment. Rub together to release the natural oils and flavour. Add the flour, butter and salt. Beat on medium speed for 5 minutes or until the mixture has a crumb-like consistency.

Add the yeast mixture and continue to mix the dough for approximately 10 minutes or until the dough is smooth and not sticky.

Place the dough into a lightly floured bowl, cover with a tea towel, and leave in a warm place to prove for 1–2 hours (depending on the heat in the room) until the dough has doubled in size.

Turn out onto a floured work surface and roll the dough out to a 2 cm (¾ in) thickness. Cut into rounds using a 6 cm (2½ in) cookie cutter. Transfer to a lightly floured baking tray, ensuring that the rounds are at least 5 cm (2 in) apart, and cover with a clean kitchen towel. Leave in a warm place to prove for a further 1 hour.

Pour some sugar onto a dinner plate for coating the cooked bomboloni. Heat the oil in a deep-fryer or large saucepan over medium heat, until it reaches 160°C (320°F) or until a cube of bread dropped into the oil turns golden in 30 seconds. Fry the bomboloni, in batches, until crisp and golden all over. Remove and drain quickly on paper towel then roll immediately into the sugar to coat.

Place your desired filling into a piping bag fitted with a round-tip nozzle and fill each bombolino.

Enjoy immediately.

15 g (½ oz) dried yeast

175 ml (6 fl oz) of warm water

zest of 1 lemon

zest of 3 oranges

85 g (3 oz) sugar

450 g (1 lb/3 cups) plain (all-purpose) flour

75 g (2¾ oz) butter, cut into cubes and softened

½ teaspoon salt

canola or sunflower oil for deep-frying

sugar, for coating

a few tablespoons of your choice of filling (custard, jam, etc)

Makes 16
CHOCOLATE PEANUT-BUTTER BROWNIES

This was the first recipe I'd ever come across that paired salt with chocolate, that's how far back it goes. We use smooth peanut butter because I don't think the chunks are necessary here, but crunchy peanut butter will work just as well.

Preheat the oven to 150°C (300°F). Grease and flour a 25 cm x 35 cm (10 in x 14 in) baking tin.

Melt the chocolate and butter together in a heatproof bowl set over a saucepan of simmering water. Stir until smooth and combined.

In a separate bowl, sift the flour, salt and baking powder together. Mix to combine well.

In another bowl, mix the eggs, vanilla extract, sugar and coffee together with a wooden spoon until combined. Stir in the melted chocolate, then fold in the dry ingredients and the chocolate chips and mix until it all comes together into a gloriously sticky mixture.

Pour into the prepared baking tin. Drop dollops of the peanut butter onto the top and, using a butter knife, swirl lightly onto the surface of the brownie mixture.

Bake for 35 minutes. The brownie will still appear a little wobbly, but don't worry, it will set further as it cools. Allow to cool completely before cutting into squares.

500 g (1 lb 2 oz) dark chocolate

450 g (1 lb) unsalted butter

195 g (7 oz) plain (all-purpose) flour

pinch of salt

1 teaspoon baking powder

2 extra-large eggs, lightly beaten

1 teaspoon vanilla extract

380 g (13½ oz) sugar

1 tablespoon instant coffee granules

100 g (3½ oz) chocolate chips

185 g (6½ oz) peanut butter, warmed

Serves 10-12

FLOURLESS CHOCOLATE HAZELNUT CAKE

This is a simple recipe which showcases its main ingredients, so it's important to use the best-quality chocolate and hazelnuts that you can afford.

Preheat the oven to 150°C (300°F). Grease and line a 23 cm (9 in) cake tin with baking paper.

Melt the chocolate and butter together in a large heatproof bowl set over a saucepan of simmering water. Stir until smooth and combined. Remove from the heat and stir in the brandy and the coffee. Add the egg yolks and whisk to combine.

In a separate bowl, beat the egg whites until peaks begin to form. Gradually add the sugar and whisk for another minute. You should have a beautiful, thick, satiny meringue mixture. Set aside.

Slowly mix the hazelnut meal into the chocolate mixture until combined. Gently fold in the meringue until just incorporated.

Pour into the prepared tin and bake for about 2 hours or until a skewer inserted into the centre comes out with a few crumbs on it. Turn out onto a wire rack to cool completely.

To make the ganache, place the chocolate and glucose into a heatproof bowl. Gently heat the cream in a saucepan over medium heat (but do not boil). Pour the hot cream over the chocolate and glucose. Let sit for 2 minutes then stir until smooth.

When the cake has cooled, pour the ganache over the top and sprinkle with the crushed hazelnuts.

375 g (13 oz) good-quality dark cooking chocolate (at least 53% cocoa solids), broken into pieces

300 g (10½ oz) butter, cut into cubes

2 tablespoons brandy

60 ml (2 fl oz/¼ cup) espresso coffee

7 egg whites

9 egg yolks

300 g (10½ oz) sugar

300 g (10½ oz) hazelnut meal

150 g (5½ oz) roasted hazelnuts, crushed

GANACHE

225 g (8 oz) good-quality dark cooking chocolate (at least 53% cocoa solids), broken into pieces

½ tablespoon glucose syrup

250 ml (9 fl oz/1 cup) thickened (whipping) cream

Makes about 10
LADIES' ARMS

This is a larger, sweet version of Ladies' fingers (page 114). Be generous with the sugar syrup.

In a bowl, combine the ricotta, sugar and rosewater.

Remove the filo pastry from the packet and cut the roll in half. Unroll both bundles and stack them on top of each other. Cover the pastry with a damp tea towel to stop it from drying out.

On a clean work surface, place three layers of pastry in a vertical strip and two layers in a horizontal strip, to form a crucifix shape. Spoon 1 heaped tablespoon of the ricotta mixture onto the intersection of the pastry.

Fold the horizontal ends in to enclose the sides, then, starting at the shortest end near the filling, bring the vertical strip over the ricotta and roll away from you to form a thick cylinder shape.

Repeat with the remaining pastry and ricotta mixture.

Pour the sugar syrup into a baking dish (you will need this after the pastries are cooked).

Heat the oil in a deep-fryer, or in a medium-sized saucepan over high heat, until it reaches 175°C (345°F) or until a cube of bread dropped into the oil turns brown in 20 seconds. Carefully fry the ladies' arms in batches for 1 minute or until crisp and golden. Drain on paper towel.

Transfer immediately to the baking dish and roll in the syrup until completely coated. Transfer to a serving platter and sprinkle with pistachios, and dried rose petals, if desired. Drizzle a little extra sugar syrup over the top.

Eat immediately.

500 g (1 lb 2 oz) fresh ricotta

1 tablespoon sugar

1 teaspoon rosewater

1 x 375 g (13 oz) packet filo pastry

canola or sunflower oil for deep-frying

100 ml (17 fl oz/2 cups) Rosewater sugar syrup (see page 168), plus extra for drizzling

50 g (1¾ oz) crushed pistachios

edible dried rose petals, to garnish (optional)

Makes about 40 pieces

BAKLAWA

Another one of Manera's delicious dishes. The difference between Greek baklava and Lebanese baklawa is that the Lebanese use cashews and rosewater whereas the Greeks use walnuts and honey. Both are delicious, but my mum's baklawa really is the winner.

Preheat the oven to 220°C (430°F). Generously grease a 30 cm x 20 cm (12 in x 8 in) baking tin with butter.

Remove the filo pastry from the packets and unroll each into a separate pile. Take the first pile and place it into the tin. Trim the pastry to fit the tin, then remove and set aside. Take three sheets of pastry from the second pile and centre it in the tin. You will have pastry hanging over the sides, but do not trim, let it hang over. Brush the top layer with melted butter. Place another three sheets on top and brush that top layer with butter. Repeat until the second pile of pastry is finished. Spread the cashews evenly over the pastry then fold the overhanging pastry inwards so it lines up with the edges of the tin.

Repeat the above process with the first, trimmed, stack of pastry, placing three sheets down and brushing with melted butter. Repeat until that pile is also used up, but do not brush the top layer of pastry with butter.

Using a sharp knife, cut the pastry into vertical strips, about 2.5 cm (1 in) wide, cutting right through to the bottom of the tin. Then cut the strips on the diagonal, to create diamond shapes. Pour any remaining melted butter over the top.

Turn the oven down to 150°C (300°F) and bake for 30 minutes or until golden.

To make the sugar syrup, combine the sugar with 625 ml (21 fl oz/2½ cups) of water in a saucepan over medium heat and bring to the boil. Simmer gently for around 20 minutes or until the syrup has thickened. Stir in the lemon juice and rosewater then remove from the heat. Set aside to cool. (This makes about 500 ml/17 fl oz/2 cups of syrup.)

Remove the baklawa from the oven and pour the syrup over the top. Sprinkle with the crushed pistachios. Leave to cool completely before serving.

This baklawa will keep in an airtight container for up to 2 weeks.

---

2 x 375 g (13 oz) packets filo pastry

250 g (9 oz) unsalted butter, melted

250 g (9 oz) unsalted cashew nuts, crushed

30 g (1 oz) pistachios, crushed

ROSEWATER SUGAR SYRUP

800 g (1 lb 12 oz) sugar

1 tablespoon lemon juice

1 tablespoon rosewater

ZUCCHINI & WALNUT CAKE

This is inspired by a Mario Batali recipe and is essentially an Italian teacake. You don't really taste the zucchini (courgette) – you probably wouldn't even guess it was in there, but it adds a lovely moistness and texture to the cake.

Preheat the oven to 150°C (300°F). Grease and line a 17 cm (6¾ in) square cake tin with baking paper.

Place all of the ingredients into a bowl and mix with a wooden spoon

Pour into the prepared tin and bake for 1 hour and 15 minutes or until a skewer inserted into the centre comes out clean.

Remove from the oven and flip onto a cake rack to cool. If you're having trouble dislodging the cake from the tin, it helps to place a wet cloth over the tin while it's sitting upside-down on the rack. Let it sit for a few minutes before lifting the tin off – the coolness of the cloth will help to loosen the cake a little.

To make the icing, bring the cream to the boil in a saucepan over medium heat. Remove from the heat and whisk in the white chocolate, stirring until melted and smooth. Set aside to cool. In a separate bowl, beat the cream cheese until smooth. Gradually add the cooled cream mixture to the cream cheese, beating to combine. Add the vanilla extract and zest and beat until smooth.

Once the cake has completely cooled, cover the top with lashings of icing and enjoy.

1 large zucchini (courgette), grated

250 g (9 oz) sugar

230 ml (8 fl oz) olive oil

250 g (9 oz) crushed walnuts

¼ teaspoon ground cloves

¼ teaspoon ground nutmeg

250 g (9 oz/1⅔ cup) self-raising flour

4 eggs, lightly beaten

LEMON CHEESECAKE ICING

50 ml (1¾ fl oz) thickened (whipping) cream

75 g (2¾ oz) good-quality white chocolate, broken into pieces

250 g (9 oz) cream cheese, softened

½ teaspoon vanilla extract

zest of 1 lemon

Makes 6

LEMON TEA CAKES

These tangy treats are moist and delicious. They also keep very well in the fridge. Tiny tea cakes are a nice change from a whole large cake or cupcakes and muffins, particularly if you only have a few friends round for morning tea.

Preheat the oven to 150°C (300°F). Grease and line the bases of six 8 cm x 5 cm (3¼ in x 2 in) mini loaf (bar) tins with baking paper.

In a bowl, mix the flour, zest and butter together until combined.

In the bowl of an electric mixer combine the yoghurt, sugar and eggs. Gradually mix in the flour and butter mixture. Don't be alarmed if the batter looks a little coarse.

Divide the batter among the mini loaf tins. Bake for 20 minutes or until a skewer inserted into the centre comes out clean.

Meanwhile, to make the syrup, combine all of the ingredients in a small saucepan with 250 ml (9 fl oz) of water and simmer over low–medium heat for 10 minutes or until thick.

While the lemon cakes are still hot, poke a few holes in them using a skewer and drizzle each cake with 2 tablespoons of the syrup. Allow to sit for a few minutes before turning out onto a wire rack to cool.

To make the glaze, sift the icing sugar into a bowl and mix in the yoghurt until smooth and glossy.

When the cakes have cooled, spoon the glaze over the tops, letting it run down the sides.

145 g (5 oz/1 cup) plain (all-purpose) flour

finely-grated zest of 4 lemons

145 g (5 oz) unsalted butter, softened

110 g (4 oz) Greek-style yoghurt

175 g (6 oz/¾ cup) caster (superfine) sugar

3 eggs

SYRUP

finely-grated zest of 1 lemon

1 cinnamon stick

150 g (5½ oz) sugar

GLAZE

110 g (4 oz) icing (confectioners') sugar

2 tablespoons Greek-style yoghurt

Serves 8–12
CRÈME CARAMEL

This is arguably my mum's signature dessert. It's a family recipe that also appeared in my Aunty Abla's cookbook and graces the table of almost every one of our family functions. It requires a bit of planning as you need to cook it the day before to give it time to set. But it's worth the time and the wait.

2 litres (68 fl oz/8 cups) milk

9 eggs

1 tablespoon whisky

1 tablespoon vanilla essence

440 g (15½ oz/2 cups) sugar

Preheat the oven to 200°C (400°F).

Heat the milk in a saucepan over medium–high heat until very hot but not boiling. Remove from the heat and set aside to cool.

Using an electric mixer or hand beater, beat the eggs, whisky, vanilla and half the sugar for about 3 minutes. Gradually add the cooled milk and continue to beat for another minute.

Sprinkle the remaining sugar into a 25 cm (10 in) wide x 10 cm (4 in) deep ring (bundt) tin. Place the tin over medium heat until the sugar melts and begins to turn a caramel colour. Remove from the heat immediately (be careful as the sugar can burn easily). Tilt the tin around to spread the caramel around evenly. Put the tin into a baking tin and slowly pour the egg mixture into the ring tin. Fill the baking tin with enough boiling water to come halfway up the side of the ring tin.

Bake for 30 minutes, then reduce the temperature to 180°C (350°F) and cook for another 45 minutes or until a skewer inserted comes out clean. Remove from the oven and run a knife around the edge of the ring. Set the tin aside to cool completely, then refrigerate overnight.

To serve, use a platter with a lip to catch the syrup. Place the platter over the ring tin and carefully flip it over. Be careful, as there will be some syrup wanting to escape.

Serves 10–12
MANERA'S APPLE CAKE

This is a brilliant cake. It forms a delicious crunchy crust on the top as it cooks, making it part crumble, part pie, part cake. It's rustic, chunky and really delicious. Like most cakes, it's best to wait until it has cooled to cut into it, but it's also ridiculously good eaten warm with ice cream.

Preheat the oven to 150°C (300°F). Grease a 26 cm (10¼ in) ring (bundt) tin.

Place all of the ingredients into a large bowl and mix until well combined. This is a dense mixture so don't be alarmed if it feels like cement.

Spoon into the prepared tin and bake for 1½ hours or until a skewer into the cake inserted comes out clean.

Remove from the oven and flip onto a rack to cool. If you're having trouble dislodging the cake from the tin, it helps to place a wet cloth over the tin while it's sitting upside-down on the rack. Let it sit for a few minutes before lifting the tin off – the coolness of the cloth will help to loosen the cake a little.

8 green apples (such as granny smith) peeled, cored and sliced into batons

3 eggs, lightly beaten

250 g (9 oz) sugar

500 g (1 lb 2 oz/3⅓ cups) self-raising flour

250 ml (8½ fl oz/1 cup) olive oil

BASICS

GARLIC PASTE

AIOLI

LABNE

HARISSA PASTE

BAHARAT

DUKKAH

PESTO

TOMATO CHUTNEY

HOLLANDAISE SAUCE

BÉCHAMEL SAUCE

TOMATO SUGO

PUTTANESCA SAUCE

LEBANESE PIE DOUGH

PIZZA DOUGH

FRESH PASTA DOUGH

POTATO GNOCCHI

SPINACH & RICOTTA
GNOCCHI

PUMPKIN & RICOTTA
GNOCCHI

CORN POLENTA

SLOW-COOKED WINTER
GREENS

PRESERVED LEMONS

PICKLED TURNIPS

CHICKEN STOCK

VEAL STOCK

GARLIC PASTE

You will find this staple in many a Lebanese kitchen fridge and I'm sure it will soon become a regular in yours. I use it for salad dressings, marinades and on hand at barbecues, or if you're like my cousin Lisa, simply spread on a piece of fresh Lebanese flatbread.

In a food processor, blitz the garlic and salt until combined and smooth. Scrape down the sides.

With the motor running, gradually add the oil in a slow continuous stream. Every so often add a small amount of the lemon juice. This will prevent the mixture from splitting.

This garlic paste will keep in an airtight container in the fridge for up to 1 month.

100 g (3½ oz) garlic, peeled

1 teaspoon salt

750 ml (25½ fl oz/3 cups) canola or sunflower oil

150 ml (5 fl oz) lemon juice

~~~~~~

Makes 400 g (14 oz)
AIOLI

There's nothing like homemade aioli and it's much easier to make than you may think. Just don't walk away while the food processor is running as the mixture may split.

Preheat the oven to 200°C (400°F).

Place the garlic on a baking tray and roast for about 10 minutes or until soft. Peel and set aside to cool.

Process the garlic, salt, egg yolks and mustard in a food processor until well combined. With the motor running, slowly trickle in the oil. The mixture should emulsify into a thick sauce.

Transfer to a bowl and stir in the lemon juice.

This aioli will keep in an airtight container in the fridge for up to 10 days.

2 unpeeled garlic cloves

1 teaspoon salt

2 egg yolks

2 teaspoons dijon mustard

250 ml (8½ fl oz/1 cup) canola or sunflower oil

1 tablespoon lemon juice

Makes 500 g (1 lb 2 oz)

LABNE

I love labne. In fact I love plain natural yoghurt. There really isn't a savoury dish that I wouldn't add it to. Labne has a salty creaminess that pairs so well with so many dishes, but it's also great just eaten with some toasted Lebanese flatbread. Mmmmmm ...

Combine the yoghurt and salt in a bowl. Rinse the yoghurt container with 250 ml (8½ fl oz/1 cup) of water in and stir into the yoghurt–salt mixture.

Spoon the yoghurt onto a large clean square of muslin (cheesecloth). Tie the corners together tightly so the yoghurt is confined by a knot. Place in a colander set over a bucket and refrigerate for 24 hours.

Undo the knot and scoop the labne into a bowl. If it's too thick stir in a little cold water.

If desired, serve garnished with olive oil and paprika. This labne will keep in an airtight container in the fridge for up to 2 weeks.

1 kg (2 lb 3 oz/4 cups) plain yoghurt

2 teaspoons salt

extra-virgin olive oil and paprika, to garnish (optional)

Makes 250 g (9 oz/1 cup)

HARISSA PASTE

Preheat the oven to 200°C (400°F).

Place the capsicums onto a lightly greased baking tray and roast for about 20 minutes, until the skins are blistered. Set aside to cool.

Soak the chillies in water for 15 minutes. Drain and discard the water.

In a small frying pan over medium heat, dry roast the paprika and the caraway and coriander seeds for 3 minutes. Transfer to a spice grinder or mortar and pestle and grind to a fine powder.

Peel the cooled capsicums, discarding the skin, seeds and pith. Place in a food processor along with the chillies, garlic, salt and spices. Begin processing, and drizzle in the oil while the motor is running. Blend until well combined.

This harissa will keep in an airtight container in the fridge for up to 3 months.

6 red capsicums (bell peppers)

6 bird's eye chillies, deseeded

2 tablespoons paprika

1 tablespoon caraway seeds

2 tablespoons coriander seeds

8 garlic cloves, roughly chopped

1 tablespoon salt

50 ml (1¾ fl oz) olive oil

Makes about 30 g (1 oz/⅓ cup)

BAHARAT

Also called Lebanese allspice, baharat is the essence of Lebanese cooking. There are numerous variations – some add chilli, others may vary the quantities – but we're pretty happy with our recipe.

Grind the whole spices to a fine powder using a spice grinder. Stir in the ground spices.

Store in an airtight jar or container.

1 tablespoon black peppercorns

1 teaspoon coriander seeds

1 teaspoon cloves

1 teaspoon cumin seeds

1 teaspoon ground nutmeg

1 tablespoon ground allspice

1 tablespoon ground cinnamon

~~~~~~

Makes about 90 g (3 oz/1 cup)

DUKKAH

Preheat the oven to 150°C (300°F).

Spread the ingredients on an oven tray and toast for 5 minutes until lightly golden.

Transfer to a spice grinder or mortar and pestle, and grind to a coarse powder.

This dukkah will keep in an airtight container for up to 3 months.

120 g (4 ½ oz) hazelnuts

75 g (2¾ oz/½ cup) sesame seeds

4 tablespoons fennel seeds

4 tablespoons coriander seeds

4 tablespoons cumin seeds

2 tablespoons sea salt

4 tablespoons black peppercorns

Makes 500 ml (17 fl oz/2 cups)

PESTO

In a food processor, blend the parsley, basil, salt and a little of the oil until a paste forms.

Add the pine nuts, garlic and pepper and pulse until blended well.

With the food processor running, drizzle in the remaining olive oil and keep blending until smooth. Pulse in the parmesan.

Check the seasoning and adjust if necessary.

This pesto will keep in an airtight container in the fridge for up to 2 weeks.

200 g (7 oz) flat-leaf (Italian) parsley leaves

300 g (10½ oz) basil leaves

½ teaspoon sea salt

150 ml (5 fl oz) extra-virgin olive oil

125 g (4½ oz) pine nuts, lightly toasted

4 garlic cloves

½ teaspoon freshly ground black pepper

150 g (5½ oz) parmesan cheese, grated

Makes about 1 litre (34 fl oz/4 cups)

TOMATO CHUTNEY

In a large saucepan over medium heat, combine the sugar, vinegar, spices and bay leaves. When the mixture begins to caramelise, add the onion and cook for about 5 minutes, until soft and translucent.

Stir in the tomatoes and cook for about 15 minutes, until thick.

Set aside to cool.

This relish will keep in airtight, sterilised jars in the fridge for up to 6 months.

300 g (10½ oz) sugar

500 ml (17 fl oz/2 cups) white vinegar

1 teaspoon ground cinnamon

3 star anise

1 tablespoon mustard seeds

2 fresh bay leaves

1 kg (2 lb 3 oz) onions, roughly chopped

1 kg (2 lb 3 oz) tomatoes, chopped

Makes about 250 ml (8½ fl oz/1 cup)

HOLLANDAISE SAUCE

In a small saucepan, melt the butter or ghee.

Half-fill a separate saucepan with water and bring to a simmer. Place a heatproof bowl over the top ensuring the bottom of the bowl isn't touching the water. Add the egg yolks and vinegar to the bowl and whisk until light and fluffy. Add the melted butter in a slow stream, constantly whisking until the sauce is thick.

Stir in the salt and lemon juice.

Set aside to cool slightly. Use immediately.

~~~~~~~~~

NOTE: TO MAKE THE CLARIFIED BUTTER, GENTLY MELT 250 G (9 OZ) UNSALTED BUTTER IN A SAUCEPAN OVER LOW HEAT. BRING TO THE BOIL AND COOK UNTIL THE SURFACE IS FOAMY. SKIM AND DISCARD THE FOAM, THEN CAREFULLY POUR THE MELTED BUTTER INTO A CONTAINER, LEAVING ANY SOLIDS IN THE BASE OF THE PAN.

200 g (7 oz) clarified butter (see note) or ghee

2 egg yolks

30 ml (1 fl oz) white-wine vinegar

1 teaspoon salt

juice of ½ lemon

~~~~~~

Makes 1.25 litres (42 fl oz/5 cups)

BÉCHAMEL SAUCE

Stud the cloves into the onion.

Place the milk, the studded onion and the bay leaves in a saucepan. Bring to the boil over medium heat. Reduce the heat to low and simmer for 2 minutes.

Melt the butter in a non-stick saucepan over low heat. Stir in the flour and cook for 3 minutes or until the flour and butter are well combined and resembles wet sand.

Strain and discard the onion and bay leaves from the milk. Slowly add the milk to the flour and butter mixture, stirring constantly until thickened. Remove from the heat and add the salt and cheeses. Stir until smooth.

2 cloves

1 onion, peeled

1 litre (34 fl oz/4 cups) milk

2 fresh bay leaves

200 g (7 oz) butter

200 g (7 oz/1⅓ cups) plain (all-purpose) flour

2 teaspoons salt

100 g (3½ oz) smoked scamorza or fior di latte (fresh mozzarella), grated

100 g (3½ oz) parmesan cheese, finely grated

Makes 500 ml (17 fl oz/2 cups)

TOMATO SUGO

A classic. Use as a base for a pasta sauce or as the hero of one. Spread on a panini, wrap or pizza base.

Heat the oil in a wide heavy-based frying pan over medium heat. Sauté the onion and garlic for about 4 minutes until the onion is translucent. Add the bay leaves and cinnamon and continue cooking for about 3 minutes to infuse the flavours.

Using your hands, roughly crush the tinned tomatoes as you add them to the frying pan along with any liquid from the tin. Mix to combine. Bring to the boil, cover and simmer for 30 minutes.

Season to taste.

Use immediately or allow to cool and store in an airtight container in the fridge for up to 5 days. Reheat gently in a saucepan before using.

100 ml (3½ fl oz) extra-virgin olive oil

1 onion, finely diced

3 garlic cloves, crushed

2 bay leaves

1 cinnamon stick

1 x 400 g (14 oz) tin whole tomatoes

~~~~~~

Makes 500 ml (17 fl oz/2 cups)

PUTTANESCA SAUCE

A traditional sauce that's never out of style. Salty, spicy and saucy. What more do you need?

Heat the oil in a wide heavy-based frying pan over medium heat. Sauté the onion and garlic for about 4 minutes until the onion is translucent. Stir in the capers, olives, anchovies and chilli and continue cooking for about 3 minutes to infuse the flavours.

Using your hands, roughly crush the tinned tomatoes as you add them to the frying pan along with any liquid from the tin. Mix to combine. Bring to the boil, cover and simmer for 30 minutes.

Season to taste (but ensure you taste the sauce before adding salt as many of the ingredients are quite salty already). Stir the parsley through before serving.

Use immediately or allow to cool and store in an airtight container in the fridge for up to 5 days. Reheat gently in a saucepan before using.

100 ml (3½ fl oz) extra-virgin olive oil

1 red onion, finely diced

4 garlic cloves, crushed

50 g (1¾ oz) capers

50 g (1¾ oz) pitted kalamata olives

3 anchovy fillets

1 red chilli, deseeded and chopped

1 x 400 g (14 oz) tin whole tomatoes

1 handful flat-leaf (Italian) parsley, chopped

Makes 10–12 pies

LEBANESE PIE DOUGH

The following dough recipe is the basis for our delicious haloumi, spinach and sambusic pies (pages 45, 48 and 142 respectively). My mother Manera used to bake them for Alimentari every morning. She only stopped when she physically couldn't stand any more after a back operation. There were a few years there that we couldn't offer the pies and, needless to say, our customers weren't very happy. However, with Manera's help, the boys in the kitchen have since carried on the tradition.

Mix all the ingredients except the cold water in a large bowl. Gradually add the cold water, mixing until it comes together into a smooth, not-too sticky dough (you may not need all of the water). Tip onto a lightly floured surface and knead until the dough stops sticking to your hands. Roll into a ball, place in a lightly oiled bowl and cover with a clean damp tea towel. Place in a warm spot to prove for 1 hour. The dough should double in size.

Use immediately or wrap in plastic wrap and refrigerate for up to 24 hours.

½ teaspoon dried yeast

100 ml (3½ fl oz) lukewarm water

180 g (6½ oz) self-raising flour

180 g (6½ oz) plain (all-purpose) flour, plus extra for dusting

125 ml (4 fl oz/½ cup) olive oil

1 teaspoon salt

about 250 ml (8½ fl oz/1 cup) cold water

Makes 4 pizzas
PIZZA DOUGH

This is a fantastic pizza dough. For best results use Italian 00 flour, which is more finely ground than plain (all-purpose) flour.

Whisk the yeast with the water in a small bowl and set aside for 10 minutes or until frothy.

In a large bowl, add the flour, semolina, salt and oil and mix together until combined. Add the yeast mixture and bring together using your hands. Mix for about 2 minutes.

Tip onto a lightly-floured work surface and knead for 10 minutes until the dough is smooth and elastic.

Roll into a ball, place in a lightly oiled bowl and cover with a clean damp tea towel. Place in a warm spot to prove for 1 hour. The dough should double in size.

Meanwhile, preheat the oven to 220°C (430°F).

Divide the dough into four equal-sized pieces. On a floured surface, roll each portion out into rounds about 5 mm (¼ in) thick. Sprinkle a little semolina over four baking trays, place the dough on top and allow to prove for a further 10 minutes.

Top with your favourite toppings and bake in the oven for about 15 minutes.

25 g (1 oz) dried yeast

500 ml (17 fl oz/2 cups) lukewarm water

600 g (1 lb 5 oz/4 cups) 00 flour, plus extra for dusting

50 g (1¾ oz) fine semolina, plus extra for sprinkling

2 teaspoons salt

125 ml (4 fl oz/½ cup) olive oil

Makes 1 kg (2 lb 3 oz)
FRESH PASTA DOUGH

Combine the ingredients in a large mixing bowl. Knead for about 10 minutes until the dough is smooth and elastic then roll into a ball. Cover with plastic wrap and refrigerate for 1 hour before use.

Clamp your pasta machine firmly to a clean work bench and turn it to the widest setting. Divide the dough into eight equal-sized pieces. Liberally dust the pasta machine rollers and the dough with flour. Roll a portion of the dough through the pasta machine.

Click the machine down a setting, dust the dough with flour and roll through again. Fold the dough in half and dust with flour, click the pasta machine back up a setting and roll through again. Repeat this process four times. The dough is now ready to roll to your desired thickness. Dust the dough with flour and roll through the machine, clicking down a setting each time until you reach the narrowest setting. Cut into your desired shape using a cutting attachment on your pasta machine, or using a sharp knife. You'll need to do this immediately or the pasta will dry out. Repeat with the remaining portions of pasta dough.

To cook, bring a large saucepan of salted water to the boil and cook for 3 minutes. Drain.

10 x 50 g (1¾ oz) eggs

750 g (1 lb 11 oz/5 cups) 00 flour, plus extra for dusting

250 g (9 oz/2 cups) fine semolina

pinch of salt

~~~~~~

Serves 6
POTATO GNOCCHI

Fill a large saucepan with cold water. Add the salt and potato and bring to the boil. Cook for about 10 minutes until tender. While still hot, mash the potato until very smooth (for best results use a potato ricer or a Mouli grater).

Gently mix in the parmesan, flour, eggs and yolks and season with salt and pepper. Mix gently to form a soft dough. Do not overwork.

On a lightly floured work surface, divide the dough into a few portions and roll into long sausages. Using a butter knife, cut into 2.5 cm (1 in) lengths.

Bring your sauce of choice to a gentle simmer in a wide-based frying pan over medium heat.

To cook, bring a pot of salted water to the boil. Carefully drop in the gnocchi. The gnocchi will float to the surface when cooked. Transfer the gnocchi to the sauce using a slotted spoon. Simmer for 2 minutes.

Serve topped with grated parmesan.

1 teaspoon salt

1.6 kg (3½ lb) waxy potatoes (we use Toolangi delight), peeled and chopped

50 g (1¾ oz) parmesan cheese, finely grated, plus extra to serve

200 g (7 oz/1⅓ cups) plain (all-purpose) flour, plus extra for dusting

2 eggs

2 egg yolks

1 quantity Tomato sugo or Puttanesca sauce (page 185), or other sauce of your choice

Serves 4

SPINACH & RICOTTA GNOCCHI

Spoon the ricotta onto a clean square of muslin (cheesecloth). Tie the corners together tightly so the ricotta is confined by a knot. Place in a colander set over a bucket and refrigerate overnight. This will extract excess moisture and ensure a fluffy gnocchi.

Blanch the spinach in a pot of salted boiling water. Drain and refresh in cold water. Squeeze the spinach to remove as much water as possible then blitz into a paste in a food processor.

Transfer to a mixing bowl along with the drained ricotta and stir in the salt, parmesan, nutmeg and egg yolk. Gradually add the flour and tapioca flour, mixing until it forms a smooth dough.

Grease and line a baking tray and set yourself up with a bowl of water to dip your hands into to keep them moist. Roll the dough into 2.5 cm (1 in) balls. Transfer to the baking tray and refrigerate for 1 hour.

Bring your sauce of choice to a gentle simmer in a wide-based frying pan over medium heat.

Bring a large pot of salted water to the boil, then gently place the gnocchi into the pot. The gnocchi is ready when it floats to the top. Transfer the gnocchi to the sauce using a slotted spoon. Simmer for 2 minutes.

Serve with fresh basil and grated parmesan.

260 g (9 oz) ricotta

200 g (7 oz) baby spinach

1 teaspoon salt

2 tablespoons freshly grated parmesan cheese, plus extra to serve

⅓ teaspoon freshly grated nutmeg

1 egg yolk

170 g (6 oz) gluten-free or plain (all-purpose) flour

80 g (2¾ oz) tapioca flour

1 quantity Tomato sugo or Puttanesca sauce (page 185), or other sauce of your choice

fresh basil leaves, to serve

Serves 4

PUMPKIN & RICOTTA GNOCCHI

Preheat the oven to 180°C (350°F).

Wash and dry the outside of the pumpkin. Cut the pumpkin in half and place on a greased baking tray, cut sides down. Cook for 35 minutes or until soft. Set aside to cool.

Remove the seeds and discard. Scrape the pumpkin flesh from the skin into a mixing bowl. Discard the skin and leave the flesh to cool completely.

Mix in the ricotta then spoon the mixture onto a clean square of muslin (cheesecloth). Tie the corners together tightly so the mixture is confined by a knot. Place in a colander set over a bucket and refrigerate overnight. This will extract excess moisture and ensure a fluffy gnocchi.

Transfer to a mixing bowl and stir in the salt, parmesan, nutmeg and egg yolk. Gradually add the flour and tapioca flour, mixing until it forms a smooth dough.

Grease and line a baking tray and set yourself up with a bowl of water to dip your hands into to keep them moist. Roll the dough into 2.5 cm (1 in) balls. Transfer to the baking tray and refrigerate for 1 hour.

Bring your sauce of choice to a gentle simmer in a wide-based frying pan over medium heat.

Bring a large pot of salted water to the boil, then gently place the gnocchi into the pot. The gnocchi is ready when it floats to the top. Transfer the gnocchi to the sauce using a slotted spoon. Simmer for 2 minutes.

Serve with fresh basil and grated parmesan.

1 small Jap pumpkin (kabocha squash)

260 g (9 oz) ricotta

1 teaspoon salt

2 tablespoons freshly grated parmesan cheese, plus extra to serve

⅓ teaspoon freshly grated nutmeg

1 egg yolk

170 g (6 oz) gluten-free or plain (all-purpose) flour

80 g (2¾ oz) tapioca flour

1 quantity Tomato sugo or Puttanesca sauce (page 185), or other sauce of your choice

fresh basil leaves, to serve

Serves 6 as a side
CORN POLENTA

We are often asked why our polenta is so delicious. It's full of flavour and the texture is like silk. I wasn't even a polenta fan until I tried this recipe, which I had to drag out of Paul – so if you see me, feel free to thank me. This polenta is fantastic with the Pork & veal meatballs on page 96.

6 corn cobs

250 g (9 oz) instant polenta

50 g (1¾ oz) butter

100 g (3½ oz) freshly grated parmesan cheese, plus extra to garnish

1 teaspoon salt

fresh basil leaves, to garnish

Place the corn cobs in a pot with 4 litres (135 fl oz/16 cups) of cold water. Cover, bring to the boil then let simmer for 30 minutes or until tender.

Strain the corn, reserving the liquid (this is your corn stock). Set the corn aside to cool.

Once cool enough to handle, cut the kernels from the cobs and set aside.

Heat 1.5 litres (51 fl oz/6 cups) of the corn stock in a saucepan over medium heat. Whisk in the polenta, and cook, stirring continuously, for about 2 minutes or until thickened.

Turn the heat to low then stir in the butter, parmesan, salt and corn kernels. Stir to combine then remove from the heat. Using a stick blender, process until smooth.

Garnish with grated parmesan and fresh basil leaves.

Serves 6–8 as a side

SLOW-COOKED WINTER GREENS

This simple side dish is a great accompaniment with almost anything. It's also lovely as part of a mezze or antipasto selection.

Heat the olive oil in a wide saucepan over medium heat, add the onion and garlic then turn the heat down to low. Cook for 10 minutes or until the onion is translucent and softened. Add all the greens along with 250 ml (8½ fl oz/1 cup) of water. Stir to combine.

Cover and simmer for 45 minutes, frequently stirring to stop the greens from burning. Add the chilli flakes and season to taste.

Remove from the heat and set aside to cool.

To serve, drizzle with the extra-virgin olive oil and lemon juice.

250 ml (8½ fl oz/1 cup) olive oil

2 onions, sliced

10 garlic cloves, crushed

1 bunch chicory (endive), roughly chopped

1 bunch cavolo nero (Tuscan kale), roughly chopped

1 bunch Swiss chard (silverbeet), roughly chopped

1 bunch kale, roughly chopped

1 bunch spinach, roughly chopped

2 tablespoons chilli flakes

100 ml (3½ fl oz) extra-virgin olive oil

100 ml (3½ fl oz) lemon juice

Fills 1 large jar
PRESERVED LEMONS

Place the lemons in a large bowl and cover with cold water. Leave to soak in a cool place overnight.

The next day, drain and cover again with fresh cold water. Leave to soak again overnight.

On the third day, drain off the water and, using a small sharp knife, make five slits in each lemon, cutting about halfway into the flesh.

Fill each incision with 1½ teaspoons salt, then pack the lemons into a large sterilised jar. Add the cardamom pods and bay leaves to the jar and then fill with boiling water. Cover tightly with the lid.

Store in a cool, dark place for 30 days before using. These preserved lemons will keep in an airtight container in the pantry for up to 6 months.

8 lemons
100 g (3½ oz) salt
6 cardamom pods
3 fresh bay leaves
boiling water, for filling

~~~~~~

Fills a 4 litre (135 fl oz/16 cup) jar
PICKLED TURNIPS

Mix the turnip and beetroot together and place in a large sterilised jar. Sprinkle with the salt then top with half vinegar, half water.

Allow to sit, uncovered, for 24 hours. Cover tightly with the lid, and gently turn the jar to combine the ingredients.

Refrigerate for 3–4 days before eating. After opening, these pickled turnips will keep in the fridge for up to 1 month.

3 kg (6 lb 10 oz) turnips, thickly sliced into batons

1 beetroot (beet), thickly sliced into batons

1 tablespoon salt

white vinegar, for filling

Makes 4 litres (135 fl oz/16 cups)

CHICKEN STOCK

Place the chicken bones in a stockpot or very large saucepan and cover with 5 litres (169 fl oz/20 cups) of water. Bring to the boil, skimming off the fat as it rises to the surface.

Turn down the heat, add the remaining ingredients and simmer for 1½ hours, skimming occasionally.

Strain through a sieve and set the liquid aside to cool.

This stock can be stored in the fridge for up to 5 days or frozen for up to 3 months.

2 kg (4 lb 6 oz) chicken bones

1 onion, halved

3 garlic cloves

1 leek, cut into thirds

2 celery stalks, cut into thirds

5 thyme sprigs

6 flat-leaf (Italian) parsley stalks

1 teaspoon coriander seeds

1 teaspoon white peppercorns

Makes 4 litres (135 fl oz/16 cups)

VEAL STOCK

Preheat the oven to 220°C (430°F).

Roast the bones and trotter in a baking tin for about 1 hour, turning occasionally, until browned all over. Transfer to a stockpot or very large saucepan.

Roast the vegetables and garlic in the same tin for about 30 minutes, turning occasionally, until golden. Mix in the tomato paste and roast for another 5 minutes. Transfer to the stockpot.

Remove and discard any fat left in the baking dish, then place over medium heat and deglaze with the red wine, scraping up any bits on the bottom of the pan. Pour over the bones and vegetables.

Add 5 litres (169 fl oz/20 cups) of water to the stockpot along with the thyme, bay leaves and peppercorns. Bring to the boil, skimming off the fat as it rises to the surface. Turn down the heat and simmer for 3 hours, skimming occasionally.

Strain through a sieve and set the liquid aside to cool.

This stock can be stored in the fridge for up to 10 days or frozen for up to 3 months.

2 kg veal bones

1 pig's trotter

2 carrots, chopped

1 celery stalk, chopped

1 large onion, chopped

2 garlic cloves

1 tablespoon tomato paste

500 ml (17 fl oz/2 cups) red wine

2 sprigs thyme

2 bay leaves

1 tablespoon black peppercorns

INDEX

THANKS

A huge thank you to my parents, Henry and Manera Malcolm, who have made *everything* possible for me. My mother, who, seven days a week for ten years, woke up every morning to bake our pies, and my wonderful father, who delivered them to Brunswick Street by 9 am every day. I'm eternally grateful for your ongoing love and support.

To our beautiful children, Aziza and Axel, who have tolerated Mum and Dad's absences on weekends and the never-ending 'work talk' at home. We love you.

Ashlee, the most incredible woman, business partner and bestie. I promise to never take being on the same page for granted. Ever!

Amit and Kaji for embracing everything you've learned and giving it back in spades. Thank you for your dedication, passion, positivity and enthusiasm.

Mario Fijan for being an amazing friend and support for over ten years.

To our incredible senior staff, who lead cracking teams at both Smith Street and Brunswick Street – thanks for working your butts off to ensure Alimentari continues to thrive.

Jane Willson at Hardie Grant, who saw in Alimentari what we have seen all these years. Thank you for instigating this wonderful experience.

Hannah Koelmeyer, whose patience and gentle nature helped turn Paul and Linda, restaurateurs, into Paul and Linda, recipe writers. A huge task!

Lauren Bamford and Deb Kaloper for your beautiful photos and styling.

Michael Harden for helping me string my sentences together and for your beautifully written foreword.

We've been incredibly fortunate to have crossed paths with some amazing people who have contributed to the success of Alimentari. Suppliers, past and present employees, some who stayed with us for years – that's unheard of in hospitality. I have wonderful memories of past Brunswick Street employees, and others who helped set up Smith Street Alimentari, which was a huge task and at times extremely stressful. Thank you all for your hard work, dedication, patience and enthusiasm.

Also, a big thanks to my beautiful 'fruzzes' and to Meaghan Gorski, who's given me nothing but unconditional friendship and support.

And yet, all of this would be nothing without our incredibly loyal and amazing customers, some of whom used to bring their kids in for babycinos and are now picking those same kids up after their Alimentari shifts. Thank you for still considering us your home away from home. We seriously could not have done it without you.

Linda and Paul

Published in 2016 by Hardie Grant Books

Hardie Grant Books (Australia)
Ground Floor, Building 1
658 Church Street
Richmond, Victoria 3121
www.hardiegrant.com.au

Hardie Grant Books (UK)
5th & 6th Floors
52–54 Southwark Street
London SE1 1UN
www.hardiegrant.co.uk

Additional photographs: page 9 by Lorna Hendry; page 206 by Michelle Tran

A Cataloguing-in-Publication entry is available from the catalogue of the National Library of Australia at www.nla.gov.au

Alimentari: Salads + other classics from a little deli that grew
ISBN 9781743791295

Publishing Director: Jane Willson
Project Editor: Hannah Koelmeyer
Design Manager: Mark Campbell
Designer: Julia Murray
Typesetter: Megan Ellis
Photographer: Lauren Bamford
Stylist: Deb Kaloper
Production Manager: Todd Rechner
Colour reproduction by Splitting Image Colour Studio
Printed and bound in China by 1010 Printing International Limited